THE NEW INTERNATIONAL
WEBSTER'S POCKET
BUSINESS
DICTIONARY
OF THE ENGLISH LANGUAGE

◆◆◆

D1012575

TRIDENT PRESS
INTERNATIONAL

Published by

Trident Press International

2002 Edition

ISBN 1-888777-53-2

Printed in the United States of America

abandonment *Law* The deliberate surrender of property or rights without conveying ownership to another as in abandonment of a rental property before the lease is up.

abatement *Accounting* Cancellation, all or in part, of a levy, such as for taxes, or a special assessment. *Law* Termination of a cause of action.

abend, abnormal ending *Computers* The termination of computer processing caused by a program or system fault.

ability to pay *Labor Relations* Descriptive of a company's capacity to absorb the cost of wage or fringe benefit increases demanded by a union; a company rejecting demands during contract negotiations on the basis that they cannot afford the cost may be forced to open its books to the union.

abort *Computers* To terminate the processing of data before completion.

above the line *Accounting, Finance* Any item on a financial report that affects the line, or bottom line of the report which is income before taxes, such as income subject to tax and expenses that are deductible.

absorbed *Accounting* Descriptive of fixed expenses such as for rent and administration, so described because they are absorbed into manufacturing costs according to a formula based on budgeted units. The condition of a fixed expense that has been completely charged off to manufacturing cost for the accounting period. See also *absorption costing*.

absorption costing *Accounting* A method of calculating the cost of manufactured units by assigning all

1

costs to those units: variable costs are applied directly; fixed costs are assigned based on the absorption rate.

absorption rate *Accounting* The standard by which fixed costs are allocated to variable costs, as by number of units, hours of operation, etc.

accelerated depreciation *Accounting* Any of a number of systems for calculating the reduction in the book value of an asset based on a larger reduction in the early years.

access *Computers* To load a program or call up data for processing.

access code *Computers* A user's name or series of characters that are required to log onto a computer, program or certain files; a security code.

access time *Computers* The time required for a computer to retrieve information from storage or to return it to storage.

account, accounts *Accounting* The records of a company's financial transactions, grouped by type, as Assets, Expenses, Liabilities, Sales, etc. *Commerce* A company's contracts with customers and vendors, often allowing payment at a later date; the record of that contract.

accountability In general, the chain of command through which may be determined the person held accountable for an action, a project or some other phase of company activity; responsibility for some facet of the company operation.

account aging *Accounting* The classification of open accounts, receivable or payable, by the lapsed time since the transaction was recorded, usually in thirty day increments.

accountant One trained in the management of financial records and reporting of the financial aspects of an organization.

account executive *Marketing* Generally, a company executive, the primary link with a company's clients, who is often the mediator between the interests of the company and the needs of the client.

accounting The science of providing meaningful information about a company's finances as a tool for management.

accounting check *Accounting, Computers* A routine, such as totaling columns across a spreadsheet, to assure that data has been entered accurately.

accounting cycle Any set of procedures with a specific beginning and ending, such as for an accounts payable that begins with a journal entry and ends when a check is written.

accounting method The system used by a business for maintaining financial records as cash basis or accrual basis.

accounting principles Generally accepted procedures for recording and reporting financial transactions, often influenced or governed by tax law.

accounting procedure The step by step process used to record and report the financial transactions of an organization.

accounting system The means by which the financial transactions of an organization are recorded, including personnel, equipment and programs.

account number *Accounting* A numeric or alphanumeric number assigned to an account for easy reference; usually, a particular series represents a type of account, such as 1000 for Expense, 2000 for Income, etc. and numbers within the series represent subsets, as 1100 for Supplies, 1200 for Utilities, etc. *Commerce* The number that identifies the company's accounts with outside vendors or services, as a bank account.

accounts payable *Accounting* The record of amounts owed to suppliers of goods or services.

accounts receivable *Accounting* The record of amounts owed to the company for goods or services rendered.

accrual *Accounting* The accumulation of charges against accounts, whether or not anything of value is exchanged.

accrual accounts *Accounting* The records, on a company's books, of charges that are due or anticipated, as accrued liability for rent or taxes.

accrual basis An accounting method wherein payables and receivables are recorded as they are incurred, with an adjusting entry made to the ledger when they are actually paid or received. See also *cash basis*.

accumulated depreciation *Accounting* A compilation of the amount that has been charged off to depreciation that, when deducted from the original cost of the item being depreciated, shows the adjusted basis or book value of the item.

acknowledgment *Commerce*, *Law* Affirmation by signature of agreement to the terms and conditions of a contract or other document

acoustic coupler *Computers* A device that connects a

telephone handset to a computer modem.

acquisition That obtained by a company, usually to improve or expand operations, as a piece of property, another company or new equipment.

across the board Affecting everything in a group the same way, as an across-the-board price increase.

active file *Computers* A computer file visible to the user and ready for processing.

active window *Computers* The screen area where the active file is viewed.

act of God *Law* A phrase used in contracts to describe an event caused by forces of nature for which the parties to the contract cannot be held responsible.

actual cost *Accounting* The amount paid, as for equipment, as distinguished from residual value, market value or resale value.

actual damages *Law* Losses directly relating to the matter at hand and that can be corroborated, as distinguished from indirect losses, as from pain and suffering.

adapter *Computers* A device, program, or routine for making disparate hardware or software elements compatible.

adaptive system *Computers* A computer program that learns by keeping a record of corrections to its activity, such as for correcting errors in optical character recognition.

ADC, analog to digital converter *Computers* A device that converts analog signals to digital data.

add-on *Computers* A peripheral device or program to enhance performance of an existing device or program

ADP, automatic data processing *Computers* The manipulation of data with the use of a computer.

addendum Something added, as a commentary to a report or additional terms to a contract.

adjudicate *Law* To hear both sides of a dispute and render a judgment.

adjusted basis *Accounting* The cost of an asset, reduced by accumulated depreciation.

adjuster *Insurance* Employee of an insurance company responsible for evaluating and settling claims.

adjusting entry *Accounting* An account entry that corrects an earlier, incorrect entry.

administer To provide the guidance and control required for a group or organization to achieve a stated objective.

administrative expense *Accounting* Costs associated with the guidance and control of the operations of a company, such as management, accounting and general office personnel and supplies, that are not directly associated with manufacturing cost.

ad valorem Latin According to value; an assessment, such as taxes or insurance based on the value of the commodity involved.

advance A prepayment in anticipation of an obligation as against expenses, commissions or work to be performed.

advertising Any means by which an organization seeks to influence the thoughts or actions of an individual, usually used to sell a product or to promote good will.

affiliate An organization that is in some way

connected to another, as through ownership, working agreement, etc.

affirmative action Action taken to correct past discrimination by seeking to hire minorities, trade with minority vendors, etc.

after market *Commerce* The sale of replacement parts or add-ons after the original product is sold; the trade in used or recovered material or equipment. *Marketing* A target audience or audiences that may be sought for a product in addition to the primary market.

after tax *Finance* Descriptive of a value adjusted for real or anticipated tax liability, as profits after tax from company operations or an investment.

age discrimination *Law* Unfair denial of employment or employment benefits based on age.

aged accounts *Accounting* A listing of accounts, receivable or payable, in categories by date due or past due, often designated as current, 30 days, 60 days, 90 days and over 90 days.

agent One who acts as the representative of another, such as a company sales representative or an insurance adjuster.

aggregate A universe of information or things, considered as a whole, such as aggregate sales that represents all sales from all divisions of a company for the defined period.

agreement *Law* An understanding between two or more parties that is a basic requirement for a contract. *Labor Relations* The contract between employees in a bargaining unit and their employer.

agribusiness Agriculture, or farming, as a big

business, often involving company divisions or affiliates that process the farm products.

air bill Documentation for an air shipment.

air freight Commodities moved by air when speed is the overriding consideration.

algorithm A set of very precise instructions for completing a specific task. *Computers* A finite set of instructions with a distinct stopping place.

alias *Computers* A name assigned to a file, a location, a block of data, etc., used to address it for processing.

allocate, allocation *Accounting* The assignment, by formula, of fixed costs to the cost of manufactured product; the allowance for the purchase of various assets, goods and services. *Computers* The assignment of computer resources for a specific purpose, such as setting aside an area of memory for the operation of a TSR. *Manufacturing* The allotment of resources, materials and equipment time, to the fabrication of various products. *Marketing* The quota set for different products or prospects.

allowance *Accounting* Amount set aside for contingencies, as an allowance for bad debt. *Manufacturing* Time included in production standards for delays, as down time or operator fatigue. *Marketing* A rebate offered by a manufacturer to a distributor or retailer, as for advertising or promotion.

alphameric *Computers* See alphanumeric.

alphanumeric *Computers* Characters that are alphabetic or numerical, excluding symbols; short for alphabetic/numeric.

ALT, alternate key *Computers* A shift key that is

used in conjunction with another key or keys to execute a command.

ALU, arithmetic and logic unit *Computers* The part of the CPU, or central processing unit, that performs arithmetic and logic functions.

AMA, American Management Association A professional organization that publishes information and sponsors seminars for managers.

American Marketing Association A professional organization that promotes sound and ethical practices in the areas of sales, advertising and marketing.

ambiguous *Computers* Imprecise; descriptive of a program command or formula that is stated in such a way that it may yield an undesirable result.

amend To revise by correcting or modifying, as a statute or a contract.

amendment A revision or addition that serves to correct or improve.

amenity That which gives added comfort or pleasure, as a privilege or facility available to employees of a company or to those of a certain rank.

amortization, amortization schedule *Accounting* The division of debt into periodic payments that include interest and other charges associated with the debt.

analog *Computers* Descriptive of data represented as a continuous variable, such as sound.

analog to digital converter *Computers* A device that converts analog data to digital data.

analyst One who specializes in the study of various aspects of business, reports on deficiencies and makes recommendations for their improvement.

AND operator *Computers* A Boolean operator used to return a value of true if the statements it joins are both true, as in a spreadsheet formula.

annotation *Computers* An explanatory note in a program or document; a feature in some word processing programs that allows commentary within a document without changing the original document.

annualize To extrapolate data from a limited period to fit an annual model, with consideration given to highs and lows that occur throughout the year.

annual meeting Meeting shortly after the end of the fiscal year at which time the company managers report to the stockholders and members of the board of directors stand for election.

annual report *Finance* The statement of a company's finances and, often, prospects for the future.

annuity *Insurance* A type of life insurance contract that guarantees periodic payments to the insured at some future time, usually retirement.

ANSI, American National Standards Institute An organization that establishes standards affecting most industries.

antitrust *Law* Descriptive of a set of laws that regulate business to prevent monopolies, price fixing, price discrimination, etc.

anti-virus *Computers* A program or routine designed to detect unauthorized alteration of a computer program or files.

application *Computers* A computer program designed for a particular use, such as a word processor or spreadsheet; a particular use to which a program is applied, as for compiling financial transactions or inventory records.

application generator *Computers* A program or utility that assists the user in creating custom designed applications.

applied cost *Accounting* The amount of overhead expense that is charged to a department, manufacturing operation or job.

appreciate *Finance* To increase in value.

appropriation *Accounting, Manufacturing* Money or materials set aside for a specific purpose. See also *allocate, allocation.*

arbitration *Labor Relations* A means of settling disputes in which the parties to the dispute agree to present their arguments to a mutually agreeable impartial third party called an arbitrator. See also, *binding arbitration.*

architecture *Computers* The design of a computer that defines such things as type of processor, speed, bus size, etc.

archives Generally, storage for inactive records. *Computers* Database records saved as inactive files after deletion from the active database.

arithmetic expression *Computers* A formula that uses a mathematical operator and returns a numeric value.

arithmetic relation *Computers* An expression that uses a mathematical operator to show the relationship between two values, such as = (equal to), SYMBOL 185 \f "Symbol" (not equal to), > (greater than), etc.

arm's length transaction *Law* A business deal between unrelated persons or organizations in which there is no conflict of interest for either party; a measure of the legitimacy of a contract or other business arrangement.

array *Computers* An arrangement of data in named rows, columns and layers—a financial spreadsheet, for example may be a two dimensional array in which the rows represent items of expense for a company and the columns, different calendar periods; a three dimensional array might consist of layers containing similar data for various divisions or departments in the company.

arrears *Accounting* A payment that is past due.

articles of incorporation *Law* The document filed with a state that sets forth the objectives of the corporation and other information as required by law.

artificial intelligence *Computers* Descriptive of the ability of a computer to simulate human intelligence, as by recording corrections to its output and adjusting for future transactions.

artificial language *Computers* A programming language with a distinct set of rules and vocabulary.

ASCII, American Standard Code for Information Interchange *Computers* A basic system for representing printable and control characters for the microcomputer as binary digits.

as is *Commerce* An offer to sell goods in their present condition, without changes or repairs.

assembler *Computers* A program that translates a programming language into instructions that are understood directly by the computer.

assembly line *Manufacturing* A manufacturing technique that involves moving a product through a series of contiguous stations where partial assembly of a product, or a part for a product, is performed.

assembly plant *Manufacturing* Descriptive of a manufacturing operation where few, if any, of the parts used are formed internally, that is, all or most of the parts are bought from another plant or from outside suppliers, either standard or custom made. See also *fabricator*.

assessment A determination of the estimated value of property; insight into the status of a situation. *Accounting* A special charge or portion of a common expense that is charged to a company entity, as a department or division.

asset Any item of value, often descriptive of the strong points of a person or company. *Accounting* The balance sheet entries that express the worth of a company, as cash, accounts receivable, equipment, good will, etc. *Law* The property of a person or business available for discharge of debt.

assign To designate for a specific purpose, as to assign materials to a job; to delegate, as an individual to perform a task. *Law* To transfer ownership.

assignment That is assigned, as materials, resources, etc. *Law* To transfer rights, as for security for a debt; an instrument of transfer, such as a deed.

attest To affirm as true by sworn statement or signature.

attractive nuisance *Law* That which serves to draw attention and may be dangerous, especially to children, such as a pond or a vacant house.

attrition Uncontrolled loss of personnel, as by illness or retirement, or of equipment, as by wear and tear.

audience *Marketing* Descriptive of those who are considered potential buyers for a product or service; those who might be reached by a particular type of advertising; see also target market.

audio system Computer Any of the programs or devices that allow the use of a computer for the reproduction of sound or make it capable of responding to voice commands.

audit Any thorough analysis, as of a procedure or problem. *Accounting* A periodic review of a company's financial records and accounting procedures.

auditor *Accounting* One who is responsible for the review of a company's financial records.

audit trail *Accounting* The orderly recording of financial transactions so that any record in the system can be tracked back to its source.

automatic backup *Computers* A program that creates a backup copy of files as they are saved; a program that makes a copy of data in the computer at a predetermined time.

automatic link *Computers* A connection between embedded objects in documents or files that provides for the update of all instances of the object when a change is made in one.

automatic load *Computers* A program in computer memory that is brought on line by a predetermined signal, as of a timer, often used to create backup files during the night.

average cost *Accounting* The total cost to manufacture a given lot of goods divided by the number of units manufactured; the total value of a group of items in inventory, bought at different prices, divided by the number of items.

average balance *Finance* A system for calculating finance charges that calls for applying the interest rate to the total of the daily balances of the account for a set period by the number of days in the period.

axis A straight reference line on a graph, horizontal, vertical, or on a plane that is perpendicular to both the horizontal and vertical lines.

background check The process of verifying a prospective employee's references and job history.

background noise *Computers* Extraneous matter in a scanned image or in electronic transmission.

background processing *Computers* The performance of tasks by a computer without interaction with the user, such as printing a document or sorting a database, often while other work is being done in the foreground.

back haul *Commerce* The return trip of a commercial vehicle after making a delivery, often empty; see also deadhead.

backlog *Marketing* Orders received by a company that have not been filled. Backlog is often used to measure the relative strength of a company or a market by comparing the value or volume of backlog for different periods or different companies.

back pay Wages or salary owed from a prior period. *Labor Relations* Payment to employees who continue to work without a contract while negotiating; the back pay covers any increases in the new agreement, retroactive to the date of the termination of the old contract.

back up *Computers* The process of making a copy of

data for safe keeping; the copy so made.

backup copy *Computers* A copy of data files and programs held as protection against corruption of the originals.

backup system *Computers* Computer hardware designed to take over processing in the event of a failure in the primary system; the procedure for recording and manipulating data in the event of a primary system failure. A device that provides power to the computer in the event of an outage. A system of hardware and software for making a copy of the data in a computer; see automatic backup.

backward compatibility *Computers* An upgraded program's ability to use files created by an earlier version.

bad debt *Accounting* An account that is written off because it is considered not collectible; see also, reserve for bad debts.

bait and switch *Marketing* The practice of advertising a product at a very attractive price, then attempting to convince the buyer to purchase another product at a higher price.

balance sheet *Accounting* A report that shows the financial condition of a company at a specific point in time. The report lists the assets of a company, such as cash, accounts receivable, inventory and equipment, and liabilities, such as accounts payable, loans, and mortgages. The difference between the assets and liabilities is owner or stockholder's equity.

balloon payment *Finance* A final payment on an installment loan that is significantly larger than the periodic installments that include only interest and little or none of the principle. Such an arrangement is acceptable to the lender when the loan is secured by an asset of greater value than the outstanding debt and is often desirable to suit the needs of a new business that has little cash, but anticipates having it by the time the final payment is due.

bankrupt, bankruptcy *Finance* The state of being judged unable to pay ones debts. A business may be forced into a Chapter 7 or involuntary bankruptcy when creditors petition the court to appoint a trustee to manage the company finances and liquidate the company, if necessary, to protect their interests. A Chapter 11 bankruptcy is the result of a petition by the business for protection from creditors while it reorganizes under court supervision.

bar chart A diagram that shows quantities as columns of varying length according to their relative magnitude.

bar code *Computers* A pattern of vertical stripes of varying widths representing codes that can be read by a scanner and recorded by a computer. Commonly used to identify consumer products at the point of sale, bar codes are also applied to mailing pieces for automated sorting and in manufacturing operations to identify raw materials, operation codes, employee time cards, etc. See also, *shop floor collection, Universal Product Code*.

bargaining agent *Labor Relations* An organization or individual authorized to negotiate pay scales, fringe benefits, working conditions, etc. with an employer as the sole representative of a group of workers comprising a bargaining unit.

bargaining unit *Labor Relations* A group of employees who have elected to bargain with management as a single entity through a duly elected representative and, by a majority vote, to accept or reject any offer made to them through their representative. See also, *collective bargaining*.

base pay The regular hourly wage of an employee, exclusive of overtime pay, shift differential or fringe benefits.

BASIC, Beginner's All-purpose Symbolic Instruction Code *Computers* A programming language.

basis *Accounting, Finance* The cost at which an asset is carried on the company books, and that is the number used to calculate depreciation for tax purposes. Such basis includes the cost of the asset itself, and in the case of equipment, may also include the cost of delivery and installation.

batch *Computers* A set of files or commands that are processed as a unit.

batch command *Computers* A single command that causes the execution of a number of commands contained in a batch file.

batch file *Computers* A program file containing a series of commands that are processed in order.

batch processing *Accounting* A cost accounting technique in which an item is manufactured in batches, expressed in pounds, gallons, units, etc. and costs are compared based on final output. See also *job processing*. *Computers* Processing of data that, once started, takes place without further input from the operator, as contrasted to interactive processing.

baud *Computers* A measure of transmission speed over telephone lines.

BBS, Bulletin Board Service *Computers* A message center that may be accessed by computer users via telephone lines.

before tax *Finance* Descriptive of a value that has not been adjusted for tax liability, as before tax profits from company operations or an investment.

benchmark A clearly defined standard for comparison, as for a value or performance; benchmark testing involves comparing results, such as the timed operation of a computer, with known results of a specific unit's performance when processing identical material to that used in the test.

benefit Anything that improves conditions; see fringe benefits. A company sponsored event to raise money or goods for a worthy cause.

biannual Descriptive of an event that takes place twice a year; semiannual; see biennial.

bid bond *Commerce* A guarantee in the form of a certified check, surety bond, or similar instrument by a person or company bidding, as a contractor for construction or manufacturing work, or for the purchase of goods. The bid bond is required to offer some assurance that the bidder is financially sound, or as protection to the party seeking bids for costs incurred by default of the bidder.

bi-directional printer *Computers* A computer printer head that prints while traveling in either direction across the paper, thus improving output speed.

biennial Descriptive of an event that takes place once every two years; see biannual.

billing cycle *Accounting* The precise procedure of reporting and recording transactions from the original sale to the rendering of an invoice or statement to the client. The time between periodic billing for the sale of goods or services.

bill of lading *Commerce* The record of goods transferred to a common carrier for delivery to a third party, expressing the contract between shipper and carrier.

bimonthly Once every two months; of that which occurs six times a year.

binary code *Computers* The representation of characters by the use of the binary system.

binary digit *Computers* The digits in a binary system, 0 or 1.

binary logic *Computers* A type of reasoning in computer formulae that returns one of two possible variables, as true or false, yes or no.

binary system *Computers* A number system in base 2.

binder *Law* A temporary agreement or contract, usually for some consideration, pending execution of a formal contract, such as a binder on an insurance policy or real estate that protects the buyer until a contract can be drawn.

binding arbitration A means of settling disputes in which the parties to the dispute agree to present their arguments to a mutually agreeable impartial third party called an arbitrator and agree to be bound by his or her decision.

BIOS, Basic Input/Output System *Computers* That part of the operating system that controls communication between the various elements of the computer and peripherals.

bit *Computers* Short for binary digit, the basic unit in the binary system.

bit mapping *Computers* The creation of a graphic image composed of tiny dots, or pixels, each of which is assigned a series of bits to record its precise location.

B/L or b/l See *bill of lading*.

blacklist A list of individuals or organizations considered undesirable for employment, transacting business, etc.

bleed *Colloq., Commerce* To charge at an excessive rate. *Finance* To take money, often illegally, from the working capital of an organization.

blister pack A firm, clear, bubble of plastic, often shaped to conform somewhat to that of the product it contains, affixed to a rigid backing, usually used for small items sold from hanging racks. See also, *shrink pack*.

block *Computers* A section of data, files, etc. that are manipulated as a unit.

block command *Computers* An instruction that acts on all elements in a particular section of text or files.

blue collar *Manufacturing* Descriptive of industrial workers, without regard to skills.

blue laws Any local ordinance that prohibits the conduct of business on a Sunday.

blue pencil To revise or edit, as a report.

blueprint An architect or engineers drawing; a type of printer's proof. Any detailed plan of action.

board of directors A group of individuals, elected by

boilerplate

the stockholders of a corporation, responsible for appointing the chief executive officers and monitoring their performance.

boilerplate *Law* A preprinted contract form, as for a lease or a sales contract.
Standardized language in a contract listing terms, rights and obligation of each party, etc.
A standard contract used by a company for its sales or lease agreements.

bomb *Computers* A situation wherein the computer locks up and must be restarted.

bond *Commerce* A contract wherein a bonding agency guarantees payment for specific goods damaged in storage or in shipment, or for the dishonest or careless act of an employee. *Finance* An interest bearing document used as a means for the government or business to raise money. *Law* A written obligation to guarantee performance.

book *Accounting* To confirm a transaction by recording it.

bookkeeper *Accounting* One who records accounting transactions for a business.

bookmark *Computers* A user-inserted reference marker in a data file that allows instant return from another location.

books *Accounting* Collectively, the accounting records of an organization, as journals and ledgers.

book value *Accounting* The cost of an asset, reduced by accumulated depreciation.

Boolean algebra *Computers* A system of calculation used in computer programming based on Boolean logic.

Boolean logic *Computers* A logic system used in computer programming based on a return of one of two variables, as true or false, yes or no.

boot *Computers* The act of starting up a computer by loading the operating system, called a *cold boot*. Restarting once the operating system has been loaded is called a *warm boot*.

bootleg software *Computers* A program obtained outside of normal channels, such as proprietary software transferred illegally to a second user.

bootstrap *Computers* A disc or device that loads the operating system onto a computer, enabling it to function.

bottom line A brief summary of a situation or report. *Accounting* Net profit or loss.

boycott To refuse to traffic with a particular organization or product and to encourage others to follow suit; often an organized effort to punish, or bring pressure to bear for the correction of perceived wrongs.

brainstorming A meeting open to the expression of all ideas, however bizarre, for the solution to a specific problem, without evaluating their merit. Later, the suggestions are evaluated and a plan of action is established. Often used to describe any discussion of a problem solving nature.

branch *Computers* A command to jump to another section of a program; an unconditional branch directs a move to a specific location; a conditional branch first calls for a test, then directs a move when certain conditions are met.

branch, branch office Any facility at a distance from

the main plant or home office of a company.

brand *Marketing* A distinctive mark used by a company to identify its products.

brand loyalty *Marketing* A measure of the extent to which a consumer will seek out and repeatedly purchase a particular brand of a product.

brand manager *Marketing* An executive responsible for the advertising and marketing of one of a company's brands.

brand name The unique name of a particular product. Usually used to infer a well-known product.

BRC, business reply card A response card, usually with postage paid, designed for convenience so as to elicit maximum response from the consumer.

breach A break, as of a violation of the law or of a contract.

breach of contract *Law* The wrongful violation, or breaking, of a contract, as by not fulfilling a promise contained in the contract, by disclaiming the duty to perform, by illegally assigning any part of the contract, etc.

breach of promise The breaking of a promise, usually undocumented.

breach of trust *Law* A violation of duty by a trustee, as through fraud or carelessness.

break even analysis *Finance* A technique for establishing the point at which income equals expense. Calculations may involve an estimate of overhead and operating expense for a given period to determine how much income must be generated over that same period in order to break even. Based on units of production, the cost of materials, manufacturing and overhead is weighed against the number of units to determine selling price per unit; when the market determines selling price, fixed costs, such as overhead and set up are the deciding factors, defining how many units must be manufactured and sold to cover costs.

break-even point *Finance* The level of production or sales at which all costs are recovered. Once fixed cost is recovered, only variable cost is incurred for additional units, so that additional sales at the same price will produce a profit. See also, ***marginal cost***.

BRE, business reply envelope A response vehicle, self-addressed, often postage paid, furnished to a client or prospect in hope of a timely reply.

budget Generally, a detailed plan for a measured period, setting goals and outlining resources needed to meet those goals. *Accounting* A projection of anticipated sales and expense for an organization; a projection of costs associated with an acquisition; a projection of cash flow. *Manufacturing* A projection of manpower or material needs for a given level of production; *Marketing* A sales projection; an estimate of cost for the advertising and promotion of a product.

buffer *Computers* An area of memory reserved for holding signals received or to be transmitted in order to compensate for variance in transmission speed and operation of different devices. See also, ***print buffer***.

bug *Computers* A malfunction in computer processing, caused by a program error, a read/write error or a fault in the CPU, a connector or a peripheral device.

building code The regulations established in local

ordinance that govern structural requirements, as for building materials, plumbing, electricity, etc.

building permit A license granted by a local government to erect or modify a particular structure.

bundled *Computers* Descriptive of computer hardware and software sold together as a package.

burden of proof *Law* The responsibility of a party to a law suit to substantiate the items of contention that are the basis for the suit.

bus *Computers* The collection of lines along which data travels.

business An enterprise established to provide a product or service in the hope of earning a profit. Such an enterprise may be a sole proprietorship, a partnership or a corporation.

business cycle Generally, the regular alternation of periods of prosperity and periods of recession in industry. *Accounting* The period, often one month, for which reports that measure the performance of a business are tendered and compared with other like periods. The period, usually one year, during which a business normally passes through a complete cycle of busy and slow periods.

business ethics Descriptive of a standard of ideals in the conduct of business: that of dealing in an honest manner with suppliers and customers.

business etiquette The manner in which one person deals with another in a business setting, not so different from a private setting, such as the exercise of courtesy and punctuality.

business interruption insurance Security against possible loss by the temporary closing of a business, as by fire, usually covering continuing overhead expense as well as lost profits.

buyback An agreement to accept the return of goods held on consignment. *Finance* Corporate purchase of its own stock in order to reduce the outstanding shares on the market.

buyer's market Generally, a condition that exists when supply exceeds demand so that quantities are plentiful and prices are low. In business, often descriptive of a situation in which a particular seller must attract a buyer in order to dispose of overstock, fill in production down time, generate cash flow, etc.

buy in Financial backing in return for at least partial control of the operation of a business. *Colloq.* Acceptance of an offer to take part in a joint venture.

buyout Purchase of a business or of a controlling interest in a corporation's stock.

buy-sell agreement An agreement between individuals that a business, partnership interest, etc. will be traded contingent on something, as the death of one of the parties to the agreement. Such an agreement may allow a key employee or remaining partners to buy out a deceased partner's interest instead of dissolving the partnership.

buzz words Slang that is native to a particular business or group, often meaningless outside the group. *Marketing* Words or phrases that reflect a current fad and so are used in advertising and promotion.

byproduct Anything incidental created in the course of doing something else. A byproduct may be an incidental benefit that grows out of a discussion or it may be a harmful substance generated in the course of a manufacturing or processing operation. Often byproducts are turned to good use, as the recovery of silver from spent photographic film or animal feed from the processing of grain.

byte *Computers* A basic data unit manipulated by the computer, usually eight bits.

by the book Descriptive of a management or operating style that adheres strictly to the rules, written or understood, often said of one with very rigid standards or of cautious management intent on avoiding liability or any hint of impropriety.

cable Computer The transmission link between devices in a computer system.

cache *Computers* A buffer, or special area of memory in the computer, for holding frequently called data.

CAD/CAM, Computer Aided Design/Computer Aided Manufacturing *Computers* A program that assists in planning and production.

CADD, Computer Aided Design and Drafting *Computers* a graphics program that assists in the creation of engineering drawings.

CAL, Computer Augmented Learning *Computers* The reinforcement of learning with the use of special computer programs.

calendar year The calendar dates from January 1 to December 31, as distinguished from fiscal year.

call report A record maintained by salespersons, customer service personnel, and others, of contacts with clients and prospects.

cancellation clause A provision in a contract for cancellation in certain circumstances or if certain conditions are not met, as a building contract contingent on securing financing.

capacity *Computers* The size of a computer storage device; of the ability of a computer to handle a particular task. *Law* Designating as having legal authority or competence. *Manufacturing* The potential volume of output under a given set of circumstances, as by number of shifts, number of days, total capacity or available capacity.

capital *Finance* Money or property used in the conduct of a business. See also, **assets**.

capital account *Accounting* The ledger account that represents the difference between assets and liabilities of a business.

capital asset *Finance* Property that represents a long term investment, such as buildings, land, machinery, etc.

capital budget *Finance* Monies set aside for investment in capital assets, such as new equipment, plant expansion, etc.

capital gain *Finance* Profit from the sale of a capital asset. In the case of depreciable property, such as machinery, the profit is the difference between the sale price and the book value of the property.

capital improvement An addition or upgrade to equipment or building that increases its value by improving productivity or extends its useful life. *Accounting* An expense that is added to the basis of the asset improved and depreciated.

capital intensive Descriptive of an industry that requires a substantial investment in equipment in proportion to the amount of labor necessary for manufacturing. See also, *labor intensive*.

capital investment *Finance* Cost of acquiring a business or purchasing buildings and equipment.

capitalism The economic system in which the means of production are privately owned and operated for profit that accrues to the owners.

Cartesian coordinates *Computers* Numbers that locate a point in space on a two or three dimensional array.

cash basis *Accounting* A system for reporting company finances whereby transactions are recorded as they are executed, so that Sales reflects only monies received and Expenses only monies paid out. See also, *accrual system*.

cash budget *Finance* An estimate of anticipated receipts and cash requirements for a specified period.

cash cow *Colloq.* Descriptive of a profitable business, one that generates a significant flow of cash with little effort.

cash discount A discount in the price of goods, offered for payment on delivery or within a brief, specified time.

cash flow statement *Finance* A summary of receipts and payments for a given period, reporting the availability or shortage of cash.

cashier's check *Finance* An instrument of payment generally considered the same as cash; it is drawn on the bank's own funds and signed by an officer of the bank.

cash order An order for merchandise accompanied by payment for that merchandise.

cash position *Accounting* The amount of cash or other

assets of a company that can be readily converted to cash available at a given time.

cash reserve *Finance* Cash or readily converted securities distinct from that required for immediate needs, held for contingencies.

casual labor Descriptive of individuals who perform services on an unscheduled, part-time basis. Individuals hired for a single project, as for yard or dock work and often paid from petty cash are an example of casual labor, though changes in the tax law have made it necessary, in many cases to put the casual laborer on the payroll, especially if it is someone who is repeatedly employed.

casualty insurance Protective coverage for an individual or business against losses by a sudden, unexpected or unusual circumstance, such as fire, flood, theft, etc. See also, *liability insurance*.

casualty loss *Accounting* A property loss caused by misfortune that is not covered by insurance. The expense of the loss is booked, as by recording the book value of anything destroyed and the cost of repairs, then reducing the total loss by the amount paid on the insurance claim.

cause of action *Law* The facts in a matter and the legal grounds that form the basis of a right to seek redress in a court of law. See also, *right of action*.

caveat emptor *Latin* Let the buyer beware—an admonition to a buyer to check the merchandise, price, terms, etc. before committing to a purchase.

CD, compact disk *Computers* A digital disk from which data is read by the use of a laser.

CD ROM, compact disk read-only memory A

compact disk containing data that cannot be altered.

cell *Computers* The area that holds a unit of information, such as a spreadsheet cell.

central buying The purchasing of all or part of the materials and supplies for a company's outlets, divisions or departments through a main purchasing office in order to secure and control quality, price and delivery.

CEO, chief executive officer The senior executive of an organization, appointed by the board of directors, with ultimate responsibility for the attainment of corporate goals.

certificate of incorporation The legal document that attests to the existence of a corporation, stating its name, purpose, financial structure, etc.

certificate of occupancy A document issued by a local government affirming that a building complies with local codes and is fit for occupancy.

certification To confirm as authentic or true. *Labor Relations* Official recognition of a union or other bargaining agent as the authorized representative of a bargaining unit.

certified check *Finance* A check for which the issuing bank guarantees payment by certifying that there are sufficient funds available in the account on which the check is drawn to cover it.

certified mail Mail for which a record of mailing and delivery is established by the postal service; written verification may be requested by the mailer. See also *registered mail.*

certified public accountant See *CPA.*

CGA, Color Graphics Adaptor *Computers* An early

standard for the display on a color monitor screen.

chain of command Informally, the hierarchical structure of a business from those with the most authority to those with the least.

chairman of the board The highest ranking officer in a corporation; one who presides over meetings of the board of directors.

character *Computer* Any of the set of letters, numbers and punctuation marks that can be duplicated from the computer keyboard.

character code *Computer* A set of binary digits that represents a specific symbol.

character pitch *Computer* The number of characters per inch of a type font.

character recognition *Computer* Identification of text or special printed symbols by any one of a number of input devices, such as a scanner.

character string *Computer* A set of characters processed as a unit.

chart *Computer* To create a graph that shows the relationships among a group of associated values; the graphic representation of those values; to diagram the steps in a procedure.

chart of accounts *Accounting* An organized list of the accounts in the *general ledger* or a *subsidiary ledger* of a company. The accounts are numbered in the order they appear on a financial statement and are listed in number order. Generally, a number series represents a class of accounts, as 1000 for assets, 2000 for liabilities, etc. with numbers for individual accounts assigned in such a manner as to leave room for future additions.

chip *Computer* A semiconductor in which an integrated circuit is formed.

chattel Any tangible, movable item of personal property.

chattel mortgage The pledge of personal property as security for an obligation, as money owed.

check A negotiable instrument, that calls for a bank to pay the amount shown from the maker's account. See also *cashier's check, certified check*.

checkoff *Labor Relations* A system whereby union dues is deducted from member's pay and paid directly to the union by the employer.

check protector A device that embosses the amount on a check making it difficult to alter. Also called a *check writer*.

check register A journal for recording checks as they are written, deposits to the checking account, and keeping a running balance of the amount in the account.

check signer A device for mechanically signing checks, used when the volume of checks would make hand signing a difficult task.

chose in action *Law* The right to sue for recovery of an intangible asset, as a debt.

churning *Law* Excessive trading in a client's account to generate commissions without concern for the client.

circuit *Computers* A complete path for the flow of electrical current that includes a power source, a conductor such as copper wire, a switch for engaging and disengaging the circuit, and a load or resistance.

civil law The body of law established by a state or nation; law protecting the rights of individuals.

click *Computers* To press and release a mouse button in order to position the cursor or make a selection.

client A customer; anyone who purchases goods or services from a company; an individual represented by a lawyer, accountant, etc.

clip art *Computers* Line art, borders, symbols, etc. saved on a computer disk that can be used to embellish a document, as a flyer or newsletter.

clone *Computers* A computer or peripheral that emulates the operation of a well-known brand, usually at less cost and often without any loss of quality.

close *Accounting* To complete the recording of transactions prior to summarizing the financial activity for an accounting period; to *close the books*. *Marketing* To complete a sale or sales agreement.

closed corporation *Finance, Law* A corporation whose stock is owned by one person or a few people, usually members of a family or of management.

closed loop *Computer* A programmer's error in which output modifies input, so that a final value is never reached, such as a spreadsheet formula in cell *B* that calls for the value of *A+B* and that cannot be attained, as *B* changes each time the command is executed.

closed shop *Labor Relations* An organization where only workers who are members of the union may be hired; forbidden by the Taft-Hartley act of 1947. See also, **open shop, right to work, union shop**.

closed corporation *Finance* A company, the stock of which is held by a few owners and seldom traded.

closely held corporation *Finance* A company in which most of the voting stock is held by a few shareholders although enough is publicly owned to provide a market in the stock.

closing costs *Finance* The cost of transferring ownership in real estate from seller to buyer, such as for legal fees, title search, insurance, filing fees, etc.

closing entry *Accounting* The journal entry at the end of a period to transfer the balance of an income or expense account to *earnings* in order to summarize the net difference between income and expense on owner's equity. The closing entry sets the balance of the income and expense accounts to zero, and ready to accept entries for a new period.

closing inventory *Accounting* The aggregate value of all materials and supplies on hand at the close of business at the end of an accounting period.

COBOL, common business oriented language *Computers* A high level programming language which syntax resembles spoken English and is therefore relatively easy to understand.

COD, cash on delivery The requirement that the cost for materials or services must be paid by the buyer at the time of delivery, often including a delivery charge and, if a third party is responsible for delivery and collection, often a service charge. COD terms are used mostly when the value of the sale is too small to warrant opening an account, when the sale is to a new, unknown or one time buyer, or the creditworthiness of the buyer is in question.

code A particular body of law or regulations of a political entity, as a city or state, encompassing a single subject, as for building construction or motor vehicles. *Computer* To write a program or formula in terms that the computer understands as commands or that can be translated into terms that the computer understands.

code, code word Generally, any symbol or group of symbols that represent something else. A *customer code*, for example, may tell geographic location, credit terms, type of business, etc.

code of ethics A statement of the standards of conduct to which those in a particular profession should aspire, often part of the credo of a professional society.

codicil Generally, any addition or supplement to a document. *Law* An addition to a will that adds to or alters provisions contained in the will.

coding of accounts *Accounting* The initial assignment of an identification number to each account for which financial transactions are recorded. Often used to describe the writing of account numbers on *source documents* prior to making journal entries. See also, *chart of accounts*.

coinsurance *Insurance* An insurance plan that limits the liability of the insurer, usually to a percentage of the total value of the property or of the loss; in effect, causing the insurer to cover the balance of any losses. Insurance coverage provided by more than one insurer, with each accepting a portion of the risk.

COLA, Cost of Living Adjustment A correction in wage or pension scales, usually linked to the **Consumer Price Index**, to compensate for changes in the cost of living.

cold boot *Computers* Restarting a computer that has been completely shut down.

collateral *Commerce, Finance* Property offered as security for a loan or other obligation, as buying on credit.

collect call A telephone call charged to the called party; such a call is placed through an operator who identifies the calling party and determines that the party called will accept the charges before releasing the line to the caller. See also, ***person-to-person call***.

collection *Finance* The conversion of *accounts receivable* into cash. Generally, descriptive of the process of managing the receivables of a company to insure that monies owed are collected in a timely fashion and that accounts past due are not overlooked. Turning accounts over to a company department or division, or an outside agency that specializes in collecting obligations that are past due.

collective bargaining The good faith negotiations between the bargaining agent for a group of employees and their employer or the employer's agent for the purpose of setting wage rates, fringe benefits, working conditions, etc.

collusion *Law* To conspire with another for the purpose of engaging in an illegal activity.

column *Accounting, Computers* The vertical arrangement of data in a two or three dimensional array, as for a spreadsheet.

command *Computers* A key word that activates a set of instructions for the computer. One line of program code that comprises a single instruction to the computer.

command character *Computers* A character that expresses a program control function.

command driven *Computers* Descriptive of an interactive computer program that acts on each command by the user as it is issued.

command line *Computers* The position at which instructions are entered by the user to direct processing.

commercial Descriptive of that done for profit. *Manufacturing* Designating of a lower grade or quality, that provided in bulk for reprocessing.

commercial bank *Finance* A financial institution charted by the federal government or the state in which it conducts business, allowed wide latitude in the services it may offer, specializing in commercial loans and demand deposits.

commercial credit *Finance* Open account transactions between companies doing business with each other.

commercial law *Commerce* The regulations that address the rights and responsibilities of persons engaged in commerce or trade, as the Uniform Commercial Code.

commercial paper *Finance* Short-term notes issued by large, financially sound corporations to cover temporary shortages in cash flow. The instrument offers cash to the issuer at interest usually below the bank rate, while the investor is afforded a safe investment for temporarily idle cash.

commercial property Real estate designed or

converted for use by a commercial establishment, as a store, factory, office, etc. Acreage zoned for commercial use.

commission A fee, often a percentage of the value of a transaction, paid to an employee or outside agent for services performed, especially a salesperson. An order to perform a service, as by an independent writer, designer or architect. An agency of the government that is charged with a particular regulatory task, as the Equal Employment Opportunity Commission or the Federal Communications Commission.

commitment A promise to do something in the future, as an employer's promise of a raise or promotion when certain conditions are met; a written agreement to buy certain goods or services at a specific price. Dedication or involvement, as a company's commitment to quality.

committee A group of individuals, usually appointed, assigned to meet for a particular purpose, as a *grievance committee*, assigned to hear and judge the worth of alleged wrongs in the workplace, or a *quality committee*, charged with the ongoing review of quality control standards and testing. Membership in a committee is often rotated to assure its vitality and generate new thinking. The committee is often given broad powers to investigate and to call in outside experts. A committee appointed to address a single, specific problem and then disband is called an *ad hoc committee*.

common carrier A person or company available for hire to transport people or goods.

common law *Law* A system of jurisprudence based on custom and court precedent, as distinguished from that based on statute.

common stock *Finance* An equity share in the ownership of a company that gives the owner the right to participate in electing the board of directors and voting on other matters brought before the stockholders, in proportion to the number of shares held. See also, **preferred stock**.

communication buffer *Computers* A device that provides temporary storage of data to be sent or as it is being received, to allow for differences in the speed of various devices.

communication link *Computers* Hardware or software that allows the transfer of data between devices.

communication protocol *Computers* Standards for the transfer of data between devices.

communication software *Computers* A program that enables the transfer of data between modems.

community property *Law* Assets accumulated by a married couple during the time of their marriage.

commuter An individual who travels regularly between two points that are a significant distance apart. Generally used to describe an individual who lives in one community and works in another, traveling the distance between them twice each day.

company A group of people joined together for a common purpose, as a business enterprise.

company car A vehicle owned by a company for the use of employees on official business. Often a vehicle owned by the company that is assigned to a particular employee for his or her use with little or no monitoring of its use for business or personal travel.

company union *Labor Relations* A union, sometimes formed at the behest of a company, that has no affiliation with other union groups and is considered to be largely under the control of the management of the company.

comparative statement *Finance* Financial reports, such as balance sheets or income statements, for different periods shown side by side so that they might be compared and analyzed. Such as comparison is an effective management tool and is usually a part of the annual report.

comparative negligence *Law* A principle of tort law upheld in some courts that in a suit for damages, the culpability of each party can be considered, so that in an auto accident, for example, if a car that is speeding strikes another car that ran through a red light, both drivers are at fault and the court may rule that no damages can be collected by either party. Such deliberation often involves an award of partial damage when it is determined that one party was more at fault than the other.

comparison shopping The process of elimination when buying to determine which product is the best value considering price and quality—one of the principal duties of a company purchasing agent.

compatibility The quality of being able to work well together, as of company employees. *Computers* The ability of certain devices, peripherals or programs to work with a particular computer. The ability to exchange programs and data between two computers.

compensating error *Accounting* An error of the exact amount made in both the debit and credit columns, often in different accounts, so the results look correct when, in fact, they are not.

compensation Anything that counterbalances another. *Commerce* Rebate to a customer for accepting damaged goods, or reimbursement for time and trouble involved in processing faulty material. *Insurance* Reimbursement for expenses associated with medical bills, lost work time, property damage, etc. *Labor Relations* Any remuneration to an employee for services performed, including wages, salary, fringe benefits, etc. *Law* Payment of damages to correct a wrong.

compensatory time Time off allowed a worker to compensate for overtime worked in lieu of pay for the overtime.

competent Qualified or capable, usually descriptive of an employee or of a vendor. *Law* Mentally able and mature; capable of understanding the terms of, and entering into, a contractual agreement.

competition *Marketing* Those who are selling similar products in the same market. The situation in which a number of producers are striving for the business of a number of consumers, so that no one producer or consumer can significantly alter the balance of the market.

competitive bid An offer by a vendor to sell a quantity of goods at a stated price. Often a sealed bid, opened at a specified time and date, so that all bidders are given equal consideration.

competitive strategy *Advertising, Marketing* Descriptive of any tactics to gain advantage over competition, as by cutting prices, advertising product strengths or a competitor's weakness, etc.

complete audit *Accounting* A detailed examination of a company's books including support documents and a thorough analysis of the system of internal controls.

compiler *Computers* A program that translates a high level programming language into machine language.

component An element or part, as a clause that is a *component* of a contract or a printer that is a *component* of a computer system.

compound To increase or combine; to add something that increases, as to compound a problem by adding another negative factor.

compound interest *Finance* Interest that is earned on interest, as when interest is added to a base amount so that the base amount plus interest is the amount on which interest is earned in the next period.

comprehensive Generally, descriptive of that including all or most of the relevant factors; extensive or complete. *Advertising* A layout for print media that emulates, insofar as possible, the final ad. Often referred to as a *comp. Insurance* Descriptive of a single insurance policy that covers a number of risks for a particular asset or group of assets.

comprehensive liability *Insurance* Insurance that offers a wide range of protection for negligence, as of repair or replacement for damage to property, or medical expense for injury to an individual.

Comprehensive business liability insurance protects the ownership of a company from liability incurred in the course of operating a business or for accidents on company property; *comprehensive personal liability insurance* protects the individual and the individual's household from personal liability on and off the individual's property.

compression *Computers* A technique of compacting data for more efficient storage or transmission.

compression utility *Computers* A program that compresses files for storage to save space and restores them as required for normal use.

compromise Any resolution to a disagreement between two or more parties in which each party gives up or modifies a demand.

comptroller, controller *Finance, Accounting* The principal accounting executive of an organization, responsible for auditing financial records and procedures.

comptroller general *Finance* Head of the General Accounting Office, that oversees the finances and accounting systems of government agencies.

comptroller of the currency *Finance* A federal office charged with the responsible for the chartering and regulation of national banks.

compulsory arbitration A means of settling a dispute between two or more parties that involves the services of a disinterested party, usually a professional mediator, who meets with those involved, then renders a decision that is binding on all. *Commerce, Labor Relations* Compulsory arbitration is usually opposed by both labor and management, but may be ordered by a court when a dispute between organizations, labor unions or an organization and a labor union is detrimental to the national economy.

compulsory insurance *Insurance* Any type of insurance that is required by law, as **workmen's compensation** or automobile liability.

compulsory retirement Obligatory retirement at a certain age mandated by company policy, an employment contract or a union contract. Federal law prohibits compulsory retirement at less than 70 years of age.

computer A device that stores and manipulates data according to instructions that it also stores.

computer art Artwork created with the aid of a computer.

computer driven Descriptive of a device controlled by a computer, as a machine that, once started, performs its tasks without further input from the operator.

computer game A program designed for amusement or instruction; often, a computer model that allows assessment of the effect of changes in a business situation.

computer graphics Charts, graphs, diagrams or pictures produced with the aid of the computer.

computer language Characters and symbols that are understood directly by the computer as commands.

computer system All of the hardware and software that make up a particular computer installation.

concession *Labor Relations* A special instance of allowing a deviation from normal terms of a contract, as a union waiver to the right to advance notice of a change in shift starting time, or an employers agreement to grant a special holiday. *Marketing* Special permission for another to sell a company's product. Special terms to a buyer, as the right to return unsold merchandise.

conciliation *Labor Relations* An attempt to convince both sides in a labor dispute to meet in an attempt to resolve their differences.

condition *Law* A clause in a contract that modifies in some way the terms of the contract based on a contingency.

conditional branch *Computers* An instruction in a computer program that is executed only if certain specific conditions are met.

conditional contract *Law* A contract that remains executory until a particular requirement is met, such as an agreement by a company to purchase equipment contingent on securing financing.

conditional sale *Marketing* An agreement to sell, as merchandise, with certain stipulations, such as a requirement that part or all of the invoice must be paid in advance, that the merchandise must be delivered by a certain date, or that the buyer need only pay for the merchandise sold and may return the rest.

conference A meeting of a group of individuals for discussion of a planned agenda. *Advertising, Marketing* A meeting to plan advertising or marketing strategy. A meeting with distributors to introduce a new product or a new marketing plan.

conference call A telephone call that links three or more parties, often at different locations.

confidence game A swindle dependent on gaining the confidence of the victim, as by tendering a phony invoice that looks official or a solicitation for an order that looks like an invoice.

configuration *Computers* The way in which a computer and peripherals are programmed and connected to function together.

confirmation Generally, corroboration or verification of something. *Accounting* Request by an auditor, sent to a client or vendor, to confirm that the amount owed to or owed by an organization as recorded on its books, is correct. *Marketing* Affirmation from a client that the specifications, delivery, price, terms, etc. contained in an order entered by the company are correct.

conflict of interest Descriptive of a situation in which self interest is at odds with duty, as of a public official who has jurisdiction over matters in which he or she has a financial interest, or a purchasing agent with a financial interest in one of his company's vendors.

conglomerate A corporation that owns controlling interest in a number of companies in unrelated industries. The merging of a number of diversified businesses.

connect time *Computers* The period during which a user is on line with a bulletin board service, fax, or other telephone link.

conservative Generally, descriptive of a tendency to rely on tradition or maintaining the status quo; of management that is moderate or cautious, relatively inflexible and not inclined to change.

Accounting Tending to extra care not to overstate assets nor understate liabilities and expenses, so as to not mislead investors to believe that the financial condition of a company is better than it is.

consideration Remuneration, as a fee for a service. *Law* Inducement for a contract; something of value given to fulfill a contractual obligation.

consignee An organization or person to whom something, such as merchandise, is assigned; the name on a bill of lading to whom the thing shipped is to be delivered.

consignment *Marketing* An allocation of goods or materials sent to a client for use or sale; an assignment or allotment; goods sent to a dealer for safekeeping or sale without transfer of ownership, such goods to be paid for when they are sold or returned if not sold.

consistency *Accounting* The practice of using the same procedures and basis for recording and reporting financial transactions over a long period of time in order to make valid comparisons between accounting periods as well as reliable projections for the future. *Manufacturing, Marketing* A measure of the quality of a product in that the buyer can evaluate a single unit, batch or shipment and expect the same quality in all units received.

consolidated statements *Finance* Balance sheets, income statements, etc. that include financial data of a company and all its subsidiaries. Financial statements, as for income, that combine the results of several periods, as monthly or quarterly, into a single report for the year.

consolidation The combining of two or more organizations or an organization and its subsidiaries to form a new entity. See also, *merger*. *Finance* Reporting on the finances of a parent company and its subsidiaries as a single operating unit. Consolidation requires that all transactions between subsidiaries, or the company and subsidiaries, be eliminated.

consolidator A forwarding company that combines small rail freight shipments to make up full carloads that the railroad will accept.

consortium Generally, any alliance of individuals or companies for a common good, such as a temporary affiliation of two or more companies in an enterprise requiring shared resources or a project too large for any one of the companies to complete on its own.

constant dollars *Finance* Any method of comparing financial data for different years by adjusting for difference in the value or purchasing power of the dollar from one year to the other.

construction loan A short term obligation from the bank or other lending institution to cover building costs, often paid back with the proceeds of a loan on the finished structure.

constructive receipt The tax concept that an individual must claim income when money is made available, although it may not have been received or deposited.

consultant An individual or organization hired by another organization to provide professional advice in a specified area of expertise, as personnel management, sales, manufacturing, finance, etc.

consumer Any end user of a product; often taken to be the purchaser of a product, especially by advertisers.

consumer goods Products purchased for personal or household use.

Consumer Price Index A gauge of the changes in consumer prices, determined by a monthly survey of the cost of housing, food, etc. conducted by the Bureau of Labor Statistics.

consumer protection A body of law aimed at protecting consumers from unscrupulous sellers, shoddy merchandise, etc.

container ship A seagoing vessel that carries cargo in large, standardized containers that have been loaded with merchandise and sealed at the manufacturer's facility.

context sensitive help *Computers* A feature of some applications that display on demand, a help screen with information about the feature highlighted.

contingency fund *Accounting* Generally, monies reserved to cover unpredictable expenses; an amount set aside in an acquisitions budget for unexpected costs, as for repairs or startup costs for equipment.

contingency plan A strategy or alternative to counteract the unexpected, though possible, such as a failure to secure financing for an acquisition, the failure of a new production method, etc.

contingent fee A charge for services based on their value, as for a company that reviews freight bills for errors or a lawyer suing for damages, each of whom charges a percentage of the money recovered.

contingent liability *Finance* An amount booked for

the possible incurring of an obligation for a past event, as a pending lawsuit or disputed claim. *Law* Accountability for the acts of those who are not employees, such as the negligence of an independent agent or representative.

continuous processing *Manufacturing* Descriptive of a type of operation involved in the uninterrupted flow of a specific product, as a popular food or beverage that is processed and packaged on a line designed for that one item and no others. See also *intermittent processing*.

contra-asset account *Accounting* A ledger account that reduces the value of an asset, as *depreciation*.

contract A formal agreement between two or more persons to do something or not do something—a contract requires an offer, acceptance, and a consideration. Generally referring to an agreement in writing that is enforceable by law.

contractor One who agrees to provide materials or a service to another for a set fee.

contract purchasing An agreement between buyer and seller whereby materials or merchandise is priced based on delivery of specific quantities at intervals over a span of time. Such contracts are common in instances where the buyer requires large quantities and assurance of a stable price and delivery.

contribution *Accounting* The difference between selling price and variable cost of manufacturing a product; also called *contribution to overhead and profit, marginal income,* or *marginal contribution. Manufacturing* Describing the part a particular job or operation plays in the profitability of a department or in maintaining a desirable level of production.

contributory negligence *Law* The act of an injured person that provides part of the basis for the condition that caused injury, such as a vehicle that is struck when the driver ignores a red light.

contributory pension plan A pension plan in which the cost is shared by employer and employee.

control To regulate and manage, as finances or manufacturing operations.

control account *Accounting* A ledger account that summarizes *subsidiary accounts*, as *accounts receivable* is the control account for the summation of the transactions in individual client accounts.

control character *Computers* A non-printing ASCII character that issues a command to the computer.

controllable costs *Accounting* Costs that are variable and can be changed, as cost of materials or labor, distinct from most *overhead* or *fixed cost*, as rent or utilities.

controlled company *Finance* A firm that is subordinate to another company that owns a controlling interest in it, though the amount of direct control may vary depending on the policy of the parent company.

controller See *comptroller*.

controlling interest *Finance* Descriptive of influence over more than 50% of the voting shares of a company, although actual ownership may be less if there is a significant block of stock sympathetic to and voting with those in control or if a significant portion of the shares are widely held and generally not voted

conversational language *Computers* A programming language that specifies commands which are similar to a spoken language.

conversion *Computers* The changing of a data file format to make it acceptable for a different use or for insertion in a different program. *Finance* Change of a security or negotiable instrument from one form to another. *Insurance* The right to change one type of life insurance policy for another under certain conditions contained in a provision in the insurance contract. *Law* The illegal seizure of the property of another; the exchange of real property for personal property. *Manufacturing* A change in, or updating of, equipment or systems.

conversion cost The price of change, as the charge for converting securities or an insurance policy, or the expense of new equipment.

converter *Computers* Software for formatting data to use in a different program. A hardware connector that permits linking of devices that would otherwise be incompatible, such as a telephone modem.

convey *Law* To transfer, as title to property, from one person to another.

conveyance *Law* The instrument by which title to property is conveyed from one person to another; a deed.

cook the books *Accounting, Colloq.* Descriptive of an effort to misrepresent a company's financial position by falsifying records and reports.

cooling-off period *Labor Relations* An interval for seeking a settlement to an impasse in labor negotiations during which time a union may not strike nor an employer stage a lock-out, mandated by a contract provision or a court order. *Law* The time during which an individual who has signed a purchase agreement may cancel the contract.

cooperative Any organization owned and operated by its members and formed for their mutual benefit—members share in the work, the expense and the profits of such an enterprise.

cooperative advertising, co-op advertising Retail advertising paid for in part by the manufacturer who usually prepares the advertising and pays an advertising allowance to the retailer based on volume. Advertising of two or more products in the same spot, normally different brands owned by the same company.

coprocessor *Computers* An auxiliary chip that augments the functions of the CPU.

copy *Computers* To make a duplicate, as of a file. To duplicate copy for insertion elsewhere in a document. A program command that makes a copy of a file and saves it in another location.

copyright *Law* Protection for the owner of a creative property, as a literary, musical or artistic work, mandated by federal law. Copyright law has been extended to protect computer programs as well. To insure protection from infringement, the copyright must be registered; any use of the material by another then gives the owner of the property the right to seek damages.

corner the market Descriptive of buying a sufficient quantity of a security or commodity so as to be able to control the price.

corona wire *Computers* The wire in an electrostatic printer that attracts toner to the surface of the paper.

corporate advertising Advertising by an organization to improve its public image as contrasted to selling its products or services.

corporate structure The organization of divisions and departments within a company, including the responsibilities of each, the lines of primary and secondary communication and the lines of authority.

corporate veil A reference to the fact that acts of the individual in a corporation are masked by the corporate entity, specifically referring to attempts at hiding individual action, often illegal, under the corporate shroud.

corporation *Law* A legal entity registered with the state that exists apart from its owners, but has certain rights normally limited to individuals, as the right to own property, incur debts, etc. The advantages of the corporate form are those of: limited liability to shareholders; easy transfer of ownership through the sale of stock; continuity, that is, the death of a shareholder or of all shareholders does not end the life of the corporation.

cosign To be one of two or more signers of a contract as testimony to acceptance of the liability.

cost The capital, time, exertion, etc. associated with a course of action. *Accounting* The amount to be paid for something, as an asset, material or service. The expense to manufacture a given item. *Law* Expenses charged to the losing party in a lawsuit.

cost accounting The collection, recording, reporting

and analysis of expenses associated with the manufacture of a product.

cost allocation *Accounting* The assignment of charges for overhead, supplies, etc. to various departments, machines, etc. on a reasonable basis in order to include them in manufacturing cost.

cost analysis *Accounting* A detailed review of expenses associated with the manufacture of a particular product or an operation to study means for improvement.

cost basis *Accounting* The original price of an asset, usually the purchase price plus delivery, installation, improvements, etc., used to calculate depreciation, gain or loss on the sale of the asset, etc.

cost center *Accounting* Any unit of a company to which cost may be assigned, as a machine or department.

cost effective *Finance* Descriptive of a decision, operation or procedure that is of sufficient value to warrant its price.

cost of borrowing *Finance* Referring to the interest rate on borrowed money without regard to the amount of money to be borrowed

cost of capital *Finance* The income that a business could earn on an alternate investment of similar risk.

cost of debt *Finance* Often referring to the actual dollar cost of borrowing a specific sum of money: a factor to be considered when contemplating investment in plant or equipment that will require the use of borrowed money.

cost of distribution *Accounting* The expenses

cost of goods sold

associated with moving a product from the manufacturer or distributor to the consumer. *Marketing* The expense of motivating the move from manufacturer to distributor or consumer, including advertising, price rebates, sales commissions, etc.

cost of goods sold *Accounting* An income statement subtotal that expresses the direct expense of merchandise exchanged for income, as cost of materials, direct labor, etc. *Manufacturing* The expense associated with merchandise produced over which the manager or supervisor has control. *Marketing* The expense of manufacturing a product including direct cost and a fair allocation of indirect and overhead costs.

cost of living adjustment *Labor Relations* An alteration of wages or pensions based on increases in the cost of living, often pegged to the consumer price index. Provisions for such adjustments are contained in government retirement plans, social security rates and in most collective bargaining agreements.

cost of sales See *cost of goods sold*, *Marketing* definition. *Marketing* Often used in the sense of the cost of distribution, that is, expenses that do not affect those of production, when analyzing the effectiveness of the distribution network, advertising, salespersons, etc., that are controlled by marketing.

cost plus Descriptive of an agreement to perform work at raw cost increased by an allowance for overhead and profit; such allowance is usually based on a percentage of the raw cost, a fixed rate per unit or a flat fee for the job.

cottage industry Descriptive of a small business,

often operated out of the home or a storefront, characterized by a lack of structure associated with a larger company or factory. See also, *home based business*.

council A group of people assembled for discussion, deliberation, etc.

counsel Advice tendered after discussion or deliberation; to advise. *Law* A legal advisor.

counterclaim *Law* A claim by one who is being sued, brought against the one suing Usually a response to diminish the strength of the original suit, the counterclaim is, however, an independent action seeking redress.

counterfeit *Law* An imitation made with intent to defraud, as by making a cheap facsimile of a quality product and attempting to pass it off as genuine.

counteroffer *Law* An offer in response to an offer that is not acceptable; the counteroffer is viewed as a rejection of the previous offer.

covenant *Law* A deliberate, binding agreement, as a contract or a promise incidental to a contract. *Law* A formal contract.

covenant not to compete *Law* An agreement by an individual not to engage in a particular field of endeavor, usually for a specified length of time. The agreement is generally contained in a contract of employment or for the sale of a business to reasonably protect the employer or new owner's rights to trade secrets, client lists, etc. Such agreements have been declared invalid, however, when they serve to prevent the individual from making a living.

CPA, certified public accountant *Accounting,*

Finance A licensed accountant who has passed certain examinations and fulfilled all other requirements of the state in which he or she is licensed. Though requirements vary from state to state, certification in one state is generally considered acceptable in any state.

cps, characters per second *Computers* A measure of the speed of a printer.

CPU, central processing unit *Computers* The integrated circuits that control the operation of a microcomputer.

craft *Labor Relations* A trade that requires special training and skill, often involving years of apprenticeship.

craft union *Labor Relations* A labor organization that has as its members only those practicing a particular trade.

crash *Computers* The halt of a computer, without hope of recovery except by rebooting, caused by a program or hardware failure. *Finance* A sudden, severe drop in stock prices brought about by a lack of investor confidence.

credit balance *Accounting* In a double entry bookkeeping system, a normal balance for a liability, equity or revenue account. See also *debit balance*. Overpayment, allowance, rebate, etc. to a customer's account that results in a balance in the customer's favor.

credit bureau *Finance* An organization that collects personal and financial data about individuals, keeps a file of the information, and furnishes reports to subscribers of their service.

credit memo, credit memorandum *Accounting* Notice to a customer that his or her obligation has been reduced, stating the reason and the amount, such as an allowance for returned or damaged goods, an error on the original invoice, etc. See also, *debit memo*.

creditor *Finance* One who sells to another or loans money, expecting repayment at a later time; one to whom money is owed.

credit rating *Finance* A classification assigned an individual, organization or marketable security based on an evaluation of worth, ability to meet current financial obligations and a history of doing so. Informally, an assessment of how satisfactorily one pays bills.

credit requirements *Finance* Standards set by a bank or business that a potential debtor must meet in order to offer reasonable assurance that the debt will be paid as agreed, as for an individual borrowing from a bank or an organization seeking to buy on open account.

credit union *Finance* A cooperative financial institution established by a group of people, such as members of a labor union, for the purpose of pooling savings and loaning to members.

critical path method A technique for planning complex projects that charts each operation, assigns it a time factor, and shows lines of dependency, that is, which operations must be at least partially completed before another can be started. The critical path is the shortest possible time line through the maze of operations—controlling the critical path assures timely completion.

crop *Computers* In desktop publishing, trimming off any unwanted parts of a picture, drawing or other graphic image.

cross-check Descriptive of a technique used to verify totals in a spreadsheet: rows and columns are summed, then the total of the columns is compared to the total of the rows to verify that they are the same.

CRT, cathode ray tube *Computers* A type of picture tube used as a computer monitor screen.

culpable At fault, or liable, as when one has been indifferent to the rights of others.

current In progress; at present. *Accounting* Descriptive of an account that is paid to date; not overdue.

current asset *Accounting, Finance* Assets that are likely to be converted in the present accounting period, as cash, accounts receivable, inventory, etc.

current cost *Accounting* Present worth of an asset, such as inventory; same as replacement cost.

current dollars *Finance* Descriptive of the cost of an asset that has been adjusted to reflect the changes in the value of the dollar.

current liability *Accounting* A debt that is due to be repaid within twelve months, such as accounts payable or the portion of a long-term loan that is due within the year.

current market value *Finance* The valuation of an asset at present market prices.

current ratio *Finance* A comparison of the proportion of current assets to current liabilities, a measure of a company's ability to withstand a short term setback as by a loss to inventory or accounts receivables. See also, *quick ratio*.

cursor *Computers* The line or block that marks the insertion point for text or graphics in a word processing or similar program.

cursor arrows *Computers* Arrows on the keyboard that serve to move the insertion point up, down, right or left.

cursor control key *Computers* Any key that moves the insertion point without altering the position of copy, as arrow keys, Tab, End, Home, Page Up and Page Down.

custom, customary Descriptive of practice that is usual for a particular business or industry, for example, a book printer is usually allowed to deliver, and the publisher is expected to accept, additional or less copies than those called for in an order within an agreed tolerance.

customer The buyer, or user, of a product or service.

customer service Assistance provided by an individual or a group whose duty is to maintain a line of communication between clients and elements of the company, responding to customers' requests, keeping them informed of the status of work in process, etc. In a business with a finite number of customers, customer service personnel often work closely with the sales force, and frequently act on their behalf.

cut and paste *Computers* A feature of some programs, especially for word processing, that allow copy to be removed from one location and inserted in another.

cutback The act of reducing. Any reduction, as in the labor force, scheduled overtime, or the budget for capital expenditures. A decrease in the level of production.

cutoff, cutoff date *Accounting* A time at which transactions relating to the finances of a company will no longer be considered in an accounting period, all future transactions to apply to the following period.

cycle billing *Accounting* A technique for segmenting accounts receivables so that statements sent to various groups of clients and due dates for payment are spread throughout the month. The system allows more timely posting of accounts and provides for more efficient use of resources.

cyclic, cyclical Descriptive of anything that recurs at regular intervals, as a *cyclic demand* that may describe a market for products or services that are in demand during certain seasons, or a *cyclic industry* that increases or decreases production levels at certain times of the year.

daily report Descriptive of any account or summary of activity that is issued every day to provide information about elements of a business that are volatile and critical to smooth operation. Such a report may provide an accounting of raw materials or finished goods inventory, production output or sales logged for the previous day, or a summary of cash received and dispersed.

daisy wheel *Computers* Designating a type of impact printer in which raised characters are mounted on a rotating wheel.

damages *Law* Money that is claimed to be owed, or that a court has ordered to be paid to, an injured party as compensation for loss suffered by negligence or deliberate action of another.

data Any information. *Computers* Information that is to be entered, that has been entered, or that is output from processing, of a computer program.

database *Computers* A set of like records containing related information, such as an *employee data base* that contains a **record** for every employee, with each item of data about the employee arranged in a **field** such as name, social security number, date of birth, date hired, etc.

data block *Computers* A selection of data based on a specific search criterion.

data conversion *Computers* An altering of selected data for transfer to a different program or format, as from a database file to a spreadsheet file.

data entry *Computers* The recording or updating of information to a computer file.

data field *Computers* Any of the areas in a database dedicated to a particular item of information, as a date or name.

data format *Computers* The type of data acceptable in a particular field, as date, number, alphameric, etc.

data link *Computers* A connection between computer systems that allows information sharing. A validation formula in a spreadsheet or database that limits entry of data into a cell or field based on a previous entry. A connection between documents containing similar information, that automatically updates all documents when one is changed.

data management *Computers* The process of recording and manipulating data in the conduct of a business.

data parsing *Computers* Breaking a data string down to its basic elements for conversion to another file format, as from database fields to spreadsheet cells.

data processing *Computers* The recording and management of significant information for a specific purpose.

data record *Computers* The set of fields that comprise a unique entry in a database file.

data set *Computers* A block or series of related database records.

data structure *Computers* The way in which a particular set of database records are organized.

data transmission *Computers* The transfer of information through a computer system or between computer systems.

data validation *Computers* A means for verifying that data in a field is of the correct type or magnitude, such as by checking for a date format.

date number *Computers* A numeric value that represents a specific date, as by the number of the day and month within a year or the number of days from a base date.

dba *doing business as* A qualifier that serves to more specifically identify a business entity; the business may be legally recorded in an individual's name or a corporate name, while dealing with the public under a name that more clearly identifies the product of service offered.

deadhead *Commerce* To operate a commercial vehicle without paying passengers or cargo, often of the return trip after making a delivery.

deadline Generally, the time by which something

must be done without penalty, as the latest time for completion of a task or that an offer remains in effect.

deadlock A stalemate. *Labor Relations* Often used to describe a situation in contract bargaining wherein negotiators take an opposite or contradictory stand on an issue and neither is willing to compromise.

dead time *Manufacturing* Time during which no work is being performed. Dead time, or down time, may be caused by equipment malfunction, a lack of materials, insufficient workers to run equipment or a production line, etc. Dead time may also be scheduled, such as for preventative maintenance, shutdown for scheduled holidays, vacation, etc.

dealer *Commerce* A buyer or seller; one who trades in the marketplace. A dealer may be independent, or one who is franchised or authorized to deal in a particular product or service, advertising to the public such authorization.

debenture A document attesting that money is owed to the bearer by the issuer. *Finance* An interest-bearing bond that is issued against the general credit of an organization with no specific assets pledged. Holders of such bonds issued by a corporation are creditors and therefore entitled to payment before owners or shareholders in the event of dissolution.

debit balance *Accounting* In a double entry bookkeeping system, a normal balance for an asset or expense account. See also, *credit balance*.

debit memo, debit memorandum *Accounting* Notice to a customer of a charge to his or her account,

stating the reason and the amount, such as a correction to an invoice, etc. See also, **credit memo**.
debt ratio Any of a number of means used to measure the soundness of an organization, as the ratio between total liabilities and net worth, or between long term liabilities and net worth.
debt retirement Generally, the repayment of monies owed. *Finance* The plan for systematic repayment of monies owed, usually involving the setting aside of a specific amount in each accounting period.
debt service *Finance* Descriptive of the amount set aside for the periodic payment of interest and part of the principal on outstanding obligations.
debug Generally, to remove errors in the operation of systems, processes, or equipment. *Computer* To correct the configuration of equipment or errors in a program to achieve smooth operation.
decentralization The process of removing a measure of control and decision making from a key, central location, such as a corporation's headquarters, and placing it in the hands of those closer to the element controlled. Decentralization allows the local manager or supervisor greater freedom of action and the ability to adjust more quickly to changing needs.
decertification *Labor Relations* Loss by a union of its authorization to bargain for a group of workers. Such action is taken by the National *Labor Relations* Board when a majority of the workers represented by the union vote that they no longer desire representation by that particular union.
declining balance, double declining balance

Accounting A system of accelerated depreciation that, for tax purposes, allows a larger deduction in the earlier years. The declining balance method allows depreciation at twice the straight line rate on the book value of the asset for each year until salvage value is reached. For example, a van purchased for $20,000 is expected to last five years with a salvage value of $5,000 at the end of five years. An asset with a five year life is depreciated at 20%, but declining balance allows twice that, or 40%. Therefore, the first year, $8,000 is claimed for depreciation leaving a book value of $12,000. The second year, $4,800 is claimed—40% times $12,000—leaving a book value of $7,200. The third year depreciation calculates to $2,880, but only $2,200 is allowed because the book value cannot fall below the salvage value of $5,000.

dedicated *Computers* Designating of that set aside for a specific purpose, as an area in computer memory for a control function, or a telephone transmission line for a fax.

deduction *Accounting* An amount subtracted, as an adjustment to an invoice, or an allowance for calculating taxable income.

deed *Law* A written instrument that conveys title to a property.

de facto *Latin* In fact; of a condition that exists, although it may not be official, moral, or legal. See de jure.

default Failure to do something that is required, promised or expected; commonly, the failure to make payment of principal or interest on a loan. See also,

delinquent. *Computers* Failure to issue specific instructions for the operation of a device or program.

default configuration *Computers* Guidelines or formatting for a device or program in the absence of specific instructions by the user.

defective Imperfect or faulty, as merchandise or reasoning.

deferred Put off to a later time, often by agreement.

deferred billing An agreement whereby the bill for merchandise that is shipped is delayed for a prearranged period, such as for thirty days to allow inspection of the material when it is received, or until an agreed date, that may allow the recipient to record the purchase in a later accounting period to satisfy a budgetary requirement. Such agreements are often made when merchandise is shipped in advance of need as a convenience to the shipper who lacks warehouse space.

deferred charge *Accounting* Cost that has been incurred in the current period, but that applies to the revenues of a later period and is therefore adjusted so as to withhold from current financial reports any expense that does not apply to current revenue. Such charges may be improvements to plant or equipment that will be expensed when they are put in operation.

deferred compensation Generally, descriptive of payment or an offer of payment to an employee that is not immediately available for his or her use, such as the company share of a retirement fund, stock options, etc. *Accounting* An account for recording the cost of deferred compensation in the period it is accrued so as to match it against current revenues.

deferred income *Accounting* Income received in the current period that will actually be earned in later periods, such as prepayment for a service contract that spans several years. The amount applicable to the current year is taken as income; that for subsequent years is withheld to be matched to the period for which it is reasonable to expect that expense will be incurred.

deficit Any shortfall of cash or cash equivalent, as more liabilities than assets, or more expense than income.

defunct No longer existing; out of business.

de jure *Latin* By right; existing according to law. See also, *de facto*.

delegate To name or appoint one to a particular task; to allow one the necessary authority to accomplish a purpose; one so appointed. Delegating authority downward through an organization is seen as a critical element to effective management in that it allows individuals at each level to concentrate on their primary tasks with minimal oversight of those for which they are responsible that are performed at lower levels.

delimiter *Computer* A symbol such as a comma or quotation mark, used to separate elements of information in a data string.

delinquent Failure to do that required, such as making payment on a financial obligation. Delinquent usually implies late, with anticipation that the obligation will be met; default implies permanent failure of ability or intent that may require legal action by the creditor.

delivery *Commerce* The act of transporting goods or the actual transfer of goods from seller to buyer. *Law* The irrevocable transfer of ownership of goods, services, etc. It can be important to a business to establish when the actual transfer of ownership takes place in order to determine liability in case of damage. For example, goods in transit are the responsibility of the carrier, but in the event of damage, it is necessary to know who has to file a claim and bear any losses not covered by the carrier's insurance. Similarly, it is important to verify responsibility for goods that have been purchased and held by the seller for future delivery at the buyer's convenience.

demand *Finance* A request for payment or fulfillment of an obligation. *Law* To petition a court for that which is rightful. *Marketing* The anticipated traffic in a product at a given price. The volume of a product that may reasonably expect to be sold tends to vary directly, although not necessarily proportionately, with the price asked for the product. See also, *demand curve*.

demand curve *Marketing* A graphic representation of the relationship between price and quantity: with price on one axis and quantity on the other, the normal demand curve traces an arc that shows higher demand at lower prices and lower demand at higher prices. Modern marketing, however, has often generated a demand that runs counter to the normal price-volume relationship by selling features that actually create greater demand at a higher price.

demand deposit Money that is deposited in a bank and that may be withdrawn without prior notice by check, transfer, etc.

demand note An instrument of indebtedness, payment of which may be requested at any time without prior notice. Such notes are often carried by a lending institution for a financially secure business that occasionally needs additional cash flow, requiring only that interest be paid periodically, and the note itself retired as cash flow allows.

demographics *Marketing* The population statistics that relate to lifestyle such as age, education, income, etc., used by advertisers and marketers to select media and message to target the audience for a product.

demurrage *Commerce* The charge levied by a carrier for delay beyond the time normally allowed for loading or unloading.

department Any of the units into which a company is divided to group the jobs of those engaged in related tasks.

deposition *Law* Sworn testimony taken outside of court by a stenographer, to be presented in court at the proper time.

depreciable life *Accounting* The time over which a piece of equipment is to be depreciated; the anticipated useful life of a piece of equipment.

depreciation *Accounting* An allowance for the decrease in the value of an asset due to wear and tear. Any of the systems for calculating the decrease in value of an asset, as straight line, declining balance, etc.

deregulation The rescinding of a portion of the government regulations that pertain to a particular industry with the avowed purpose of creating a more open market with increased competition.

descending sort *Computers* An alphabetical or numerical arrangement of data from the highest to the lowest.

desktop *Computers* A set of computer accessory programs that emulate items found on a desk, as a calendar, calculator or note pad.

desktop computer *Computers* A small computer designed to fit on the top of a desk. See also, *microcomputer*.

desktop publishing *Computers* The creation of graphics material, such as newsletters, flyers, charts, etc. on a microcomputer.

destructive read *Computers* A computer read-out that simultaneously erases the source file.

detail person *Marketing* A salesperson who services retailers, primarily in the grocery business, and who supervises promotions, makes certain the company's products are properly displayed, etc.

device *Computers* Any component or peripheral that is a part of a computer system.

device driver *Computers* A program that interprets instructions for the operation of a peripheral, such as a printer

diagnostic *Computers* Descriptive of a system designed to detect and isolate errors or malfunctions in a programs or equipment.

diagnostic message *Computers* An error message that indicates the source of the error.

dialog box *Computers* A panel that appears on screen as a part of a program to furnish instructions, information or to request user input.

dilution *Finance* A reduction in the book value of a share of a corporation's stock caused by an increase in outstanding shares, as by exercise of warrants or options.

digit *Computers* A symbol representing an integer in a numbering system, as 0-9 in decimal notation or 0-F in hexadecimal.

digital *Computers* Of that represented by a discrete value.

digital camera *Computers* A camera that records images in digital format for downloading and viewing on a computer screen.

digital data *Computers* Information recorded according to a system of numbers, as binary for the computer.

digital recording *Computers* The recording of sound as discrete values.

DIP, dual in-line package *Computers* Designating of an integrated circuit that can be programmed with the use of a series of toggle switches.

direct cost *Accounting* Any expense for labor, materials, overhead, etc. that can be identified directly with the manufacture of a specific product, group of products, or a service.

direct labor *Accounting* The cost of labor that can be identified directly with the manufacture of a product, group of products, or a service.

direct marketing Generally, descriptive of selling by mail, that is, addressing the selling message to a particular prospect who can order directly from the mailer. Also describes the use of the mail to deliver a selling message for a particular product that may be bought from a source other than the mailer, as a local merchant.

director Any of the members of the board of directors that guides the affairs of an organization.

directory *Computers* In a computer hierarchical file structure, a division that holds related program or data files and sub-directories.

direct overhead *Accounting* Any *overhead* expense that can be identified directly with the manufacturing operation, and ultimately with a specific product, group of products, or a service, such as the salary of a *line supervisor*, or the cost of the space occupied by a machine.

direct sales Sales by a manufacturer to the retailer or consumer; without benefit of a middleman, broker, or distributor.

disbursement Descriptive of money paid out to satisfy an obligation.

discharge *Finance* To free from a debt or other obligation, as by payment, or by failure of another party to a contract to meet an obligation. *Labor* To terminate or dismiss a worker.

disciplinary layoff *Labor* Suspension of a worker for violation of company rules.

disclaimer A conditional statement that limits liability of the party issuing the statement under certain conditions.

disclosure Generally, the release of any information that is significant and relevant to the matter at hand, and that may not otherwise be known to the other party, such as disclosure by a purchasing agent of the company that he or she has a financial interest in one of the company's suppliers. Disclosure avoids the appearance of wrongdoing, allowing the recipient of the information to weigh the information and act accordingly. For example, in the case of the purchasing agent who has a financial interest in a supplier, management may decide it is inconsequential, that the agent should be out of the loop in any transactions involving that particular vendor, or they may insist on *divestiture*. *Finance* The inclusion in a financial report of information describing any unusual transaction that is not apparent to the reader of the report and that materially affects the bottom line.

discount *Finance* An allowance to a buyer for prompt payment. Terms of a loan in which interest is deducted from the amount of the loan at the time it is made. *Marketing* An allowance paid to a dealer or merchant for buying in volume.

discovery *Law* Any procedure for gathering information before going to court, such as that of taking testimony in advance of trial. See also, *deposition.*

discrepancy An inconsistency or abnormal variance between two or more elements. *Finance* Often used to describe a variance between budgeted or anticipated cost and actual cost.

discretionary cost In an organization, an allowance for expenses that are not absolutely necessary and that can be withheld without harm to the continued operation of the organization, such as a portion of the advertising budget, certain repairs and maintenance, etc.

discretionary income See *disposable income.*

discrimination *Labor Relations* Generally, any treatment or consideration of an individual or group of individuals that differs from that accorded most others in respect to hiring, discipline, training, work assignment, promotion, etc.

dishonor *Law* Refusal to make payment, or fulfill, an obligation, as a debt or other promise.

disk *Computers* a computer storage device.

disk crash *Computers* Destruction of a disk and the data it holds as a result of the read/write head coming in contact with the surface of the disk; any disk failure, sometimes recoverable.

disk drive *Computers* The device that holds, spins and reads from, or writes to, the disk.

diskette *Computers* A floppy or removable disk.

disk formatting *Computers* A series of reference points recorded on a disk that allow orderly and rapid storage and retrieval of data.

disk fragmentation *Computers* A condition that occurs after many reads and writes to a disk in that data for a single file is scattered throughout the disk rather than being stored in contiguous sectors.

disk sector *Computers* A section of a disk track.

disk tracks *Computers* Concentric circles of a disk where data is stored.

dispatcher *Commerce* One who works for a freight company or a **consortium** of independent haulers and whose function is to control the movement of operators and vehicles for the most expeditious movement of freight.

display console *Computers* a screen where the user views data, and monitors the operation of the computer.

disposable income That portion of an individual's income left after payment for necessities; the amount of one's income that can be spent for pleasure.

dissolution A breaking up or dissolving. The termination of a business, as a corporation by vote of the stockholders, consolidation, etc.

distribution *Accounting* The assignment of income and expenses to the proper accounts. *Marketing* Descriptive of the network that moves product from manufacturer or distributor to the ultimate consumer. Statistics regarding the purchase of a product by various *demographic* groups.

distribution allowance *Marketing* A rebate offered by a manufacturer to the wholesaler, distributor, etc. for advertising and promotion.

distributor An individual or company that is responsible for moving product from the manufacturer to the retailer. The distributor may be an agent charged with dispersing a pre-sold product, as a newsstand distributor who is charged with filling store racks with current issues of magazines and returning outdated product. Or, the distributor may be a wholesaler who carries a large stock of merchandise that is sold and delivered to individual merchants.

dithered image *Computers* A pattern of black or colored dots of varying size that create the image of a full range of gray or color tones on a computer monitor screen.

diversification The venture of a company into the providing of new products or services that may or may not be related to those already provided. Diversification can be an attempt to protect or increase market share by adding related products that are carried by competitors; or it can be directed toward product areas that are entirely new to the company to offset the effect of seasonal dips, to make good use of excess cash, etc.

divestiture The act of getting rid of something, usually, to prevent a conflict of interest.

division A separated unit of a company, often operating with great autonomy, almost as a separate company.

dock *Labor* To deduct from one's pay or allowances for a particular reason, as from wages for arriving late at the job or from vacation days of the worker who has exceeded the allotted number of sick days.

document Generally, a page of data, often official. *Computers* A printed copy of information held in computer memory.

documentation Generally, instructions, verification, etc. *Computers* Information or instructions relating to a program, procedure, etc.

document reader *Computers* A device that is able to recognize an image on paper and convert it to digital data.

document retrieval *Computers* A system for identifying and retrieving data stored in the computer.

domestic corporation A corporation that operates

totally within the state in which it is incorporated.

DOS, disk operating system *Computers* a program that controls all of the basic operations of the computer.

double declining balance See *declining balance*.

dot matrix *Computers* Printing in which characters are formed by numerous dots arranged according to the pattern established for the character.

double click *Computers* Pressing and releasing a button of a mouse twice in quick succession, used to activate a selection in some programs.

double density disk *Computers* A diskette on which data is packed in order to double its capacity.

double dipping Descriptive of having two incomes, either by holding two jobs, by collecting from two retirement funds, or by collecting from a retirement fund while holding down a full-time job. Most often used to describe individuals who receive retirement or pay from two government jobs.

double-entry bookkeeping *Accounting* The system of maintaining financial records for a company in which every entry has an offsetting entry—a system of debits and credits. For example, the purchase of goods requires an entry that adds to the value of inventory that is offset by an entry to accounts payable. The effect is to create a liability in exchange for an asset so that the net worth of the company is unchanged. The system is designed to maintain an aggregate balance that allows for detection of errors and to create an **audit trail** that allows all transactions to be traced to their source.

double-sided disk *Computers* A diskette capable of

storing data on both sides.

double taxation Descriptive of the taxing of corporate profits that are distributed to shareholders as dividends where they are taxed again as income to the shareholder. The term may also be used to describe that portion of personal income that is paid out in wages to domestic help or for goods and services that will be taxed again.

double time *Labor* Twice the normal hourly labor rate; descriptive of time worked that by agreement is to paid at double the normal rate, such as work on a Sunday or holiday.

download *Computers* To load a program or data into a computer from another computer or from a storage device, such as a disk.

down payment *Commerce* An amount paid in advance of the receipt of goods. Such a payment may be a good faith deposit, insuring that goods will be picked up at a later date; a payment that cuts the lender's risk when goods are bought on credit; or the first payment for the manufacture of a custom product that will be sold for cash, in which case the down payment usually covers the immediate out of pocket cost to the supplier.

downside risk An assessment of the cost or penalty if a project or investment goes awry. Such an assessment may be made when considering an investment in new equipment or a new product line. It may also be part of the decision making process to determine a course of action, for example, weighing the cost of unpacking and repacking a warehouse full of products that are in inventory to check for a

suspected minor fault against the cost of replacing
those products if they are returned by the consumer.

down time See *dead time*.

downward compatible *Computers* Descriptive of the
ability of a program to run with data or formatting
created by an earlier version.

dpi, dots per inch *Computers* A measure of the quality of image from a scanner or printer; the more dots
per inch, the finer the image appears to the eye.

drag *Computers* To press and hold a mouse button
down while moving the cursor, thereby moving the
image under the cursor.

DRAM, dynamic random access memory *Computers*
Memory that must be constantly refreshed to be retained and that is erased when the power is off.

draw An allowance provided to a salesperson, often
for a limited time, as personal income until commissions from sales are adequate to provide a steady
income. In some cases, the draw is not charged
against commissions, but is considered a subsidy for
a training period. A true draw, however, is deducted
from commissions at an appropriate time, and the
difference paid to the salesperson. Frequently, the
draw is continued, with the drawing and commission
accounts reconciled periodically, as monthly or
quarterly.

drive *Computers* The device that moves a disk or tape
past the head that reads from, and writes to, the
storage medium.

drive designation *Computers* The letter assigned to a
drive in order to identify it.

driver *Computers* A program or routine that

translates and conveys messages between a computer and a peripheral.

drop down menu *Computers* A program feature that presents a list of options on screen when a menu title is selected.

drop shipping *Commerce* The breaking down of a large consignment of goods for shipment directly to the customer, as a retailer or consumer. In some cases, the manufacturer may handle the drop shipping of the customer's order or the customer may accept bulk shipment and perform the drop shipping.

dry goods *Commerce* Descriptive of textiles and textile products, as clothing, bedding, thread, etc.

due care *Law* The standard of reasonable conduct that is considered in judging fault for negligence—whether or not the subject exercised due care in the maintenance of property, manufacture of a product, etc.

due process *Law* The concept of the legal system and actions taken with such system to protect the rights and liberties of the individual.

dues An amount paid to maintain membership in an organization, as a labor union. Dues are primarily to cover administrative costs, that is salaries, offices, etc. for those who run the organization, although a portion may be used to cover the cost of benefits that accrue to members, such as sickness or death benefits, legal aid, etc.

dummy Generally, an imitation or substitute for the real thing. Often, a sample submitted for approval before volume production begins, as a *dummy* book from a printer to show size and construction, or a *dummy* package to assure that the product fits and can be properly displayed.

dummy corporation A corporation formed as a holding company for another company or companies and whose only function is as a buffer between the active corporation and the true owners.

dummy invoice *Accounting* An invoice for merchandise that is made in advance of the actual invoice or as a replacement for an invoice already made. A dummy invoice may be made to cover a cash order that is to be paid before shipment: the dummy furnishes documentation required by the buyer; the actual invoice that is submitted after delivery would include freight and any additional charges not picked up on the dummy invoice.

dump *Computers* To transfer the entire contents of a file to a printer, monitor or storage device.

dumping The practice of selling goods outside of the usual distribution channels, often a foreign market, for a lower than normal price and, for a reason that brings into question the ethics of the company doing the dumping. Goods may be dumped in a foreign market because they are of an inferior quality and cannot be sold domestically. Selling at a lower price in a new market may be an attempt to undermine competition. Dumping can also be a means to increase profit—if the setup cost for production is very high, additional units beyond those that can be sold in the domestic market at regular prices may be manufactured at a very small cost; those additional units can be dumped in a foreign market and priced much lower than the same product in the domestic market while still earning a significant profit because of their low price.

dun To press for payment.

duplication A repetition of effort; to do the same task twice. *Manufacturing* A repeat of effort, as moving materials needlessly or performing a test or inspection more than once. Unless duplication is desired, as a in repeated quality control check, it should be eliminated. *Marketing* Descriptive of advertising placed in such a way that the same audience is reached through different media or different elements of the same media.

durable goods *Marketing* Descriptive of goods that represent a major purchase for most households and that have an anticipated life span of more than a few years, as a washer, dryer, automobile, etc.

duress *Law* Conduct, as a threat, that presses one to do something against his or her will.

duty *Law* A legal or moral obligation, as a duty to bargain in good faith over the terms for a labor contract, or the duty of a manufacturer to exercise reasonable care to insure that the consumer who uses the product manufactured will not come to harm because of it.

early retirement Descriptive of retirement from a job before the normal retirement age or time of service. Such retirement is often an alternative to job loss in times of cutback and usually involves a reduction of monthly benefits.

earned income *Finance* Money that comes to an individual or to a company as a result of involvement in the production of goods and services, as contrasted to earnings from investment.

earnest money *Law* Cash that is tendered by a buyer to prove that he or she is in earnest about a purchase, often that of real estate. Failure to purchase, except for agreed upon contingencies, usually involves forfeiture of the deposit.

earnings *Finance* All of the money that comes to an individual or company, regardless of the source, whether earned income or from investment, usually as reported for tax purposes.

earnings per share *Finance* That portion of the total profit reported by a company for a specified accounting period that may be allotted to each share of common stock outstanding.

easement *Law* A right granted by agreement or law for limited use of land, such as a right of way, without change of ownership.

EBCDIC, Extended Binary Coded Decimal Interchange Code *Computers* A standard code for the numeric representation of alphanumeric characters.

echelon Originally, descriptive of troop formations at varying positions or levels. Used in business to describe the levels of authority and responsibility from the top management to the least of the workers.

echo *Computers* Command or information lines that are displayed, or echoed, on the monitor screen.

economical order quantity The amount of any material that should be ordered to make the best use of the firm's resources, taking into consideration such factors as price breaks for ordering in quantity, shelf life of the material, space required and available for warehousing, anticipated time that money will be tied up in the inventory, etc.

economic life *Accounting* The anticipated time that a particular piece of equipment can be operated economically, that is, the time until operation of the equipment costs more than it can earn.

economy of scale Descriptive of the potential savings to a company through an increase in size, market share, diversification, etc. For example, a company may make better use of its equipment or buy better equipment to double its output without increasing plant size or overhead, thereby reducing unit cost through growth.

edict Originally a decree or proclamation issued by a governmental authority; now used to describe any directive that specifies clearly a company position.

edit *Computers* To make changes, as additions or deletions, to a file or document.

edit commands *Computers* Commands in a program that facilitate the process of editing, such as *move, copy, paste,* etc.

edit key *Computers* Any of the special keyboard keys, such as *insert* or *delete*, used to edit text.

edlin *Computers* A line by line text editor available in DOS.

EDP, electronic data processing *Computers* Any manipulation of data by electronic means.

EEOC See *Equal Employment Opportunity Commission.*

efficiency Of the ability to make the best use of resources—money, labor hours, and materials—in the production of goods.

EGA, Enhanced Graphics Adapter *Computers* A standard for the display on a color monitor screen.

electronic bulletin board *Computers* A computer message center.

electronic mail *Computers* The transfer of messages, with the use of the computer, from one individual to another or to a group of specified persons.

electronic spreadsheet *Computer* A computer version of a worksheet with data organized in rows and columns.

electrostatic printer *Computer* A device that creates images through the adherence of a toner to charged portions of a receiver.

embargo *Commerce* Any restriction on trade, as of certain items for security reasons, or with a particular country for economic or political reasons.

embed *Computer* To fix an element from one document or file into another.

embedded commands *Computer* Program instructions that establish and maintain the appearance, position and special characteristics of a text or graphics element.

embedded object *Computer* A drawing, chart, sound recording, etc. that is fixed in a text based document.

embedded pointer *Computer* The link between an embedded object and its source file, as the link between a chart and its spreadsheet source data.

embezzlement *Law* The misappropriation of funds or property belonging to another, by who is legally charged with their care.

eminent domain *Law* The right of government to

authorize the taking of private land for public use with just compensation to the owner of the land.

employee One who works for wages or salary.

employee stock ownership plan *Labor Relations* Any program designed to encourage those who work for a company to purchase stock in the company, often through payroll deduction, or loans backed by the company, in order to develop an active interest among employees in the success of the enterprise. In extreme cases, an opportunity for employees to take control of an ailing company.

employer An individual or organization that engages others to work for wages or salary.

employment agency Any organization, public or private that specializes in matching workers with available jobs. Most private agencies require a contract from job seekers and charge a fee for their services.

employment contract *Labor Relations* A formal agreement between employer and employee, often required of an individual hired for a high level or sensitive position. Such a contract may include a covenant not to disclose trade secrets nor to seek or accept employment in a competing firm for a specified period. Some companies require a contract of all new employees, stating simply that the individual has read, understands, and is willing to comply with company rules.

emulation software *Computers* A program that directs a peripheral to imitate another, usually to improve performance, as the emulation of laser quality by a dot matrix printer.

enable, enabling *Computers* Allowing or directing to

operate, as by computer command. *Law* Provision in a law that gives officials the power to enforce the law.

encroach *Law* To intrude on the rights or property of another.

encryption *Computers* Jumbling or coding of sensitive data for security purposes.

encumbrance *Law* A lien or claim attached to real property

END *Computers* A program code indicating the final command.

End key *Computers* A cursor movement key that sends the cursor to the end of a line of text and, used in conjunction with other keys, to the bottom right of the screen, the bottom of the page or the end of the file.

end of page indicator *Computers* A command embedded in a document to indicate the end of a printed page; the sensor on a printer that signals the end of a sheet of paper.

endorsement *Accounting* Signature on the back of a check that verifies receipt of funds. *Advertisement* A broadcast statement, usually by a well-known celebrity, that attests to or implies approval of the quality of a product. *Insurance* A document that verifies a change or addition to an insurance policy, such as special coverage, beneficiary, etc.

endowment A gift of money or property to a person or institution, usually for a specific purpose.

enjoin To forbid to do something, usually with legal authority, such as the making of false claims about a product, or spreading derogatory rumors about a competitor.

enter *Computers* To add information, as text to a document, records to a database, etc.

Enter key *Computers* A function key used to signal the end of a block of copy or enable a selected command; also expressed as CR or carriage return or Return.

enterprise A business venture, usually implying an element of risk.

entity Generally, a thing that has being. In business, the legal form elected by the owner or owners, such as a sole proprietorship, corporation, partnership, etc.

entrepreneur One who organizes and operates a business, usually implying one who is willing to accept risk in the quest for profit.

entry-level Descriptive of a job in the lower echelons of a company or a career field; a position viewed as a proving ground for new employees.

envelope feeder *Computers* A device that attaches to the printer to allow the automatic feeding of envelopes for addressing.

environment *Computers* Referring to the type of operating system, the peripherals and programs that make up a computer system.

EOM, end of month End of an accounting or payment period.

Equal Employment Opportunity Commission A government body empowered to enforce the federal regulations against discrimination by employers or unions in hiring, training, promoting, etc.

equal opportunity employer An employer who

actively seeks to end discrimination in the workplace and encourages hiring, training, promotion, etc. without regard to race, creed, color, national origin, sex, etc.

equipment Machinery used in the manufacture of goods or in the performance of a service.

equipment compatibility *Computers* The quality of computers and peripherals to share data without translation.

equipment leasing The practice of procuring equipment needed for company operations through a lease arrangement rather than through outright purchase. Such lease arrangements may be available from the manufacturer or through a third party that makes a business in financing the purchase and subsequent leasing of equipment.

equity *Accounting* The aggregate of capital paid into a business plus any retained earnings. *Finance* The market value or cost of property less any liens against that property.

erase *Computers* To delete, as a block of copy or a file, from storage.

errorlevel *Computers* In a program or batch file, a value that is tested to signal a branch.

error message *Computers* A message from an operating system or program displayed on the monitor or printer indicating that an error in processing has occurred, often citing the source of the error.

escalator clause *Commerce* A provision in a long term contract that provides for a price adjustment to cover anticipated changes in the cost of labor or materials. *Labor Relations* In a labor contract, a provision for automatic increases to cover increases in the cost of living.

escape *Computers* To discontinue processing, or to return to a previous menu or operating level.

escape character *Computers* ASCII control character 027 signaled by the Escape key and used in certain program sequences to signal the start of a printer or monitor control code.

Escape key *Computers* A function key that triggers the escape command.

escape sequence *Computers* A character string prefaced by the escape code (ASCII 027) so that computer will recognize it as a command.

escrow *Law* Something of value, as money, securities or a written instrument such as a deed, placed on deposit with a third party to be held until certain conditions are fulfilled. Escrow may be a deposit of earnest money that is held until the sales agreement is executed or abandoned; a deed that is mortgage for a real estate loan, to be returned to the rightful owner when the loan is paid or declared in default; amounts paid to the holder of a mortgage for periodic expenses such as taxes and insurance; etc.

estate *Finance, Law* Generally, all of the real and personal property that a person owns. Specifically, the nature and extent of one's ownership interest in land. All that one possesses at the time of death.

estate planning *Finance* A strategy for managing property so as to legally transfer as much as possible to one's heirs by minimizing the amount that is subject to taxes, both during life and after death.

estimated liabilities *Finance* A notation to a financial

statement that recognizes a liability, the exact
amount of which is unknown, as for taxes, or an
award by a court that is being contested.

estimator Generally, one who estimates. A vital function in a company that produces a product or service package that is tailored to the needs of a project or client, as in advertising, construction or certain types of manufacturing, the estimator calculates the anticipated cost of the project for his or her company and the client.

estop *Law* To prevent or restrain one from a denial or claim that is contradicted by previous statements or acts by that person, or by earlier findings of a court.

ethics Generally, the study of standards of conduct and morality. In practice, ethics is descriptive of the conduct one may expect from a reasonable person under normal circumstances. In addition, many trade groups have established codes of ethics that address specific areas peculiar to their business or industry.

eviction *Law* The removal of a tenant from leased property for violation of the lease contract, as by misuse of the property, non payment of rent, etc.

exchange *Commerce* Barter. To give up one thing for another, usually of comparable value. Although exchange may refer to trading promises, or a promise for material consideration, it is most usually used in the world of commerce to describe the trading of goods or services, as a consumer who returns merchandise for replacement or for something else of similar value. The exchange of merchandise or services for money is normally viewed as a *sale*.

exchange rate *Finance* The official valuation of the currency of a nation in relation to that of other nations.

excise tax A domestic duty or levy assessed on the manufacture or trade of certain commodities.

exclusion That which need not, or cannot, be included. *Finance* A qualifier to a financial statement in which the auditor or preparer notes that certain items or transactions are not included in the report or have not been verified to the preparer's satisfaction. *Insurance* A disclaimer that lists items or conditions not covered by a particular insurance policy.

execute *Computer* to carry out an instruction or set of instructions. *Law* To make valid, as by signing. To complete, as by performing according to the agreement contained in a contract.

executive An administrator. Generally, anyone in a company who has significant authority and responsibility for the operation of the company. Often used to describe anyone in a company who works on salary, as opposed to an hourly wage.

executive committee A select group of high level or key management personnel in a company, often charged with the oversight of company operations and the implementation of plans to move in new directions.

executor *Law* One appointed to carry out the wishes of another for disposition of property, etc. according to the terms laid out in a will.

executory *Law* Any part of a legal contract that has not been executed, or fulfilled.

exit *Computers* A program branch that returns

control to the next higher level. To leave a sub-routine and return to the main application program or to leave an application and return to the operating system.

exit interview *Labor Relations* A conversation with an individual who has resigned. An exit interview may offer insight into employee attitudes about a particular job, a department, and the company in general. Learning why an employee is leaving and what might have induced him or her to stay can be helpful in efforts to retain key employees or to generally reduce turnover.

ex officio By right of office; with official standing. Descriptive of membership on a committee or other group within a company that is traditionally part of the job, so that formal appointment is not required, such as a seat on the executive committee that is normally filled by the person in the position of general manager.

expansion An enlargement or broadening of scope, as of a plant, product lines, etc.

expansion card *Computers* A board that is installed in the computer to provide additional memory or functions.

expansion slots *Computers* Positions in the computer reserved for the installation of expansion or control boards.

expected return *Finance* Anticipated profit from a business, a particular venture, an investment, etc. *Expected return on investment* or *expected rate of return* is anticipated income or profit expressed as a ratio or percentage of the amount invested.

expense *Accounting* Any cost incurred in the day to day operation of the business, such as payroll, materials, or supplies. *Finance* For tax purposes, any cost that is written off in the current period; all costs that are not capitalized, assigned to ending inventory, or in some other way deferred.

expense account *Accounting* Ledger accounts that record charges to the company for which money is paid out or for which a debt is incurred. A record of costs, usually incurred by salespersons or company executives, for travel and entertainment.

expiration The date beyond which an option cannot be exercised, or beyond which an agreement is no longer in force. *Insurance* The final date that an insurance policy is in force, although certain policies may have a provision for a grace period, or for automatic renewal under certain circumstances. *Labor Relations* The final date that a labor contract is in force, although most have a clause that provides for continuance of the contract in the absence of formal notice of termination by either party. *Law* A contingency clause in a contract that often specifies a period of time after which the contract is invalid if not executed, as a real estate contract with a stipulation that financing must be arranged within thirty days from the date of the contract. Such expiration may be extended by common consent of the parties to the contract. *Marketing* The final date for a special price offer, co-op advertising, etc. The expiration may be based on the date an order is placed, accepted, or executed.

exploitation To turn to productive use. *Exploitation* is often used in a pejorative sense, as for illegal use or use without reasonable compensation; however, it may also describe putting to productive use that which was formerly considered of no value, or the clever turning of an adverse condition into a benefit.

exposure *Finance* The maximum amount of capital that is at risk in a new venture, claim, lawsuit, etc. *Marketing* Of the appearance of a product before the public through paid advertisement, promotion, or free publicity.

expressed That which is clearly stated, as the terms of a warranty, in contrast to implied.

expression *Computer* A symbol or symbols that describe a mathematical operation.

express mail A special classification for letters and packages carried by the U.S. Postal Service that guarantees overnight delivery between major cities.

extended coverage *Insurance* A provision in an insurance policy that offers coverage beyond that normally included, such as a company liability policy that covers employees driving rental cars on business.

extension *Insurance* A rider that continues a policy in force beyond its normal expiration date. *Law* An agreement between the parties to a contract to allow the contract provisions to remain in force beyond the time stipulated in the contract.

external audit Generally, any review of company structure, systems or procedures by an independent party, such as a management consultant. *Finance* A review of the financial records of a company by an independent accounting firm that can render an opinion regarding the accuracy of the records.

extrapolation A technique for predicting a numerical value that is unknown based on manipulation of that which is known. For example, if the time to manufacture 5,000 units and 10,000 units of the same item, under similar circumstances, is known, and there is a setup time involved, one may determine that the time required to manufacture an additional 5,000 units is the difference between the times for 5,000 and 10,000. From this, all things remaining equal, one can predict the time it will take to manufacture any quantity.

fabricator One who builds or constructs. *Manufacturing* Descriptive of a manufacturing operation where component parts are formed internally before assembling or are sent to another plant for final assembly. See also *assembly plant*.

facade The front of a building on the outside, often denoting a false front that has been made especially attractive or imposing. Occasionally used to describe the appearance or manner of an individual who is known or suspected to be presenting a false front, as a kind person who appears gruff.

face *Computers* In desktop publishing, all of the styles of a type of a particular design; see also font.

face value *Finance* The amount for which a negotiable instrument, such as a check or bond, is written without regard to any other consideration, as creditworthiness, market value, etc. Frequently used to describe an offer, as to buy or sell, with the implication that there are other considerations that must be taken into account to determine the real value of the offer.

facility A building, area, etc. set aside for some activity, such as a manufacturing plant, warehouse, loading dock, recreation room, etc.

facsimile, fax An exact copy. *Fax* generally denotes a copy sent to a distant location by transmitting discrete data over telephone lines.

factor Generally, one who acts as an agent for another in the conduct of business, usually buying and selling. Also any of the elements that go into the production of goods and services, as capital, labor, management, and all of their constituent parts. *Finance* To buy the accounts receivable of a company at a discount, or to accept them as partial payment for a loan or advance. Factoring provides immediate cash flow or release from debt for the company while providing the factor relative security for the monies advanced.

factory A location or building where goods are produced, assembly is performed, or material is processed.

factory overhead *Accounting* Normally, all of the expenses of a company except labor and materials that are charged directly to the product. Each company has its own system, however, so that in some, factory overhead stops at the door to the factory floor, where manufacturing operations actually take place, and the cost of offices, clerical workers, managers, etc. is calculated separately. Such costs may be referred to as *front office cost*, or *sales and administrative costs.*

failure rate *Accounting* From records kept in the cost accounting system, an analysis of the frequency and duration of equipment failure, compared to productive running time. Because equipment failure also means lost labor hours and perhaps missed deliveries, the failure rate may be a key element in justifying replacement. *Manufacturing* An analysis of units failing inspection compared to total units produced. A high failure rate may call for a review of methods, materials, etc.

Fair Credit Reporting Act *Law* Legislation enacted in 1971 to protect the consumer against circulation of inaccurate or obsolete information. Under the provisions of the act, the consumer has the right to notification by a business that it is seeking credit information, the identification of the source of a report used as the basis for denying credit, certain information from the reporting agency as to content and nature of the report, correction of erroneous information, etc.

Fair Labor Standards Act *Labor Relations* Legislation originally enacted in 1938, and administered by the Wage and Hour Division of the Department of Labor, that set basic standards for minimum wages, overtime pay, and the employment of minors. Provisions that prohibit wage differential based strictly on sex are enforced by the Equal Employment Opportunity Commission.

fair market value See *market value*.

fair rate of return *Finance* Profit level at which a public monopoly, such as a utility company, is allowed to operate as determined by government regulators. An acceptable ratio of earnings to investment that is the basis on which the management of a company may judge the worth of an expansion or other investment opportunity.

fair trade *Marketing* An arrangement whereby a retailer agrees not to sell below the price set by the manufacturer for certain brand-name items. Such agreements are now illegal in most states.

fallback That which is held in reserve for a contingency. Reference to a backup plan or option that can be put into effect if the first plan doesn't work.

false advertising *Marketing* Any information from an advertiser that is untrue or misleading, especially involving price or quality of merchandise.

fan fold paper *Computers* A continuous stream of computer paper with equally spaced feed holes along the borders, perforated between pages and folded accordion-style so as to lie flat.

fast track An accelerated career path. The *fast track* may be set up by management to bring an individual or group of individuals through a series of jobs for training to quickly reach a particular level, or it may be set by an individual who jumps from job to job, securing a promotion at each level.

fax, facsimile A copy of a document sent to a remote terminal by a fax machine or computer modem over telephone lines; to send such a copy.

fax card *Computers* A controller board in a computer that enables the transmission of a facsimile.

FDA, Food and Drug Administration An agency of the U.S. government charged with approving the safety and regulating the sale of foods, medicines, cosmetics, etc.

feasibility study Examination of a proposed venture

to determine whether it is practical and potentially profitable. Depending on the project, the study may call for analysis of data from various departments within the company as well as outside consultants. For example, a proposal for development of a new product may require information about the market for the product, the plant and equipment to manufacture it, the availability and cost of materials, lines of distribution, investment required and the cost of production.

featherbedding *Labor Relations* The practice of restricting output or requiring more workers than necessary in order to protect jobs.

federalism A system of government based on the union of a number of entities in which those that are a part of the union agree to subordinate a portion of their power to the central body thus formed in certain matters of common interest.

Federal Trade Commission, FTC *Marketing* The government agency charged with the investigation of unfair trade practices, including deceptive advertising.

Federal Unemployment Tax Act Legislation that provides for cooperation between the federal and state governments in the administration of unemployment compensation.

fee Payment for professional services, licenses, etc.

feed holes *Computers* Holes along the sides of continuous feed computer paper, engaged by a sprocket wheel for feeding into the printer.

fetch *Computers* To retrieve data or a file from storage.

FICA, Federal Insurance Contributions Act Federal legislation that outlines the taxes to be paid for Social Security.

fiduciary *Law* A person or other entity that holds something in trust for another and has a legal obligation to act in the best interests of that person in all matters regarding the property thus held, as the executor of a will who is responsible for preserving assets and investing wisely, when required to do so.

field Generally, an area of endeavor, as *a career field, a business field, etc. Computers* A single fragment of information that, combined with related fields, serves to make up a record in a database. A field is usually the smallest element of significant information that one might want to use to sort or select records in a database, or to retrieve from a database. For example, in a mailing list, city, state and zip code may be included in a single field, however, each is customarily assigned to separate fields so that records can be selected by city, by state, or by zip code.

field mark *Computer* A code that signals the beginning or end of a database field.

field name *Computer* The identification of a specific field in a database record.

FIFO; first in, first out *Accounting* A system for valuing inventory that presumes materials were removed in the same order that they were entered, thus matching the cost of the oldest material with oldest revenue. In a time of rising prices, however, it has been argued that the system unfairly increases taxable income at a time when the money paid out

figurehead

for higher priced material is tied up in inventory. See also *LIFO*.

figurehead Descriptive of a prominent individual or seemingly important position that lacks authority or responsibility; often one that is controlled by others.

file An accumulation of stored information or documents, usually arranged by subject. *Computers* A collection of data or related records that is stored as a unit. *Law* To register or place on public record, a legal document, such as a deed.

file attributes *Computers* Special nature of a file for identification or protection such as read-only, archived or hidden.

file conversion *Computers* The transfer of a file's formatting codes to allow access by another program.

file maintenance *Computers* Correcting and updating files and directories to reflect the most recent data available and purging the system of outdated files.

file management *Computers* The organization and tracking of files by the operating system and the user.

file manager *Computers* A software utility designed to simplify the task of locating and organizing files.

file name *Computers* The designation that identifies a data file.

file name extension *Computers* A tag of up to three characters following a file name that aids in identification by the operating system, a program or the user.

file protection *Computers* A file attribute that identifies a data file as read-only. Setting a device on a floppy disk to make the files on the disk read-only.

file server *Computers* A computer that stores a library of program and data files for a number of users in a network.

filter *Computers* That which refines output by sifting input according to user- or program-designated criterion. User input that restricts output to a certain class or group of information. Machine controls that eliminate extraneous signals.

finance charge *Finance* The cost for buying on credit; interest. *Law* Under federal truth in lending legislation, all of the costs associated with a loan or credit sale, such as interest, service charge, finder's fee, cost of credit report, etc.

finance company An organization that specializes in lending money to consumers or businesses, or in factoring accounts receivable.

financial analysis *Finance* The study of an organization's financial records to determine its financial condition.

financial institution A bank, insurance company, or other organization that is organized to make a profit by the investment of funds.

financial planning software *Computers* A program that assists the user in budgeting, saving, investment decisions, etc.

financial statement *Finance* Any written report that purports to show the financial condition of an individual or organization. For the individual, such a report may be a simple listing of assets and liabilities. For an organization, it may include a balance sheet, income statement, cash flow statement, a report of changes in net worth.

financing The backing of an individual or organization with loans, credit, etc.

finder's fee Generally a fee paid for bringing together the parties to a transaction, such as assisting a business in finding financing, a leasing firm, clients, etc.

finished goods inventory *Accounting* Product that is completed and ready to be sold to clients. A current asset on the balance sheet.

firm Generally used to refer to any type of business organization. *Commerce* Of that which is concluded, or not likely to change, as a *firm price* or *firm order*. *Law* Any business in which the principals are not recognized apart from it; any unincorporated business.

first in, first out See *FIFO*.

first mortgage *Finance, Law* A pledging of property as security for a debt that has priority over any other liens on the same property. In the event of default, the debt owed to the holder of the first mortgage will be satisfied before any others are considered.

fiscal policy *Accounting* The plans and rules of a company that relate to budgetary and financial matters.

fiscal year *Accounting* A twelve month period, not necessarily a calendar year, chosen by the management of an organization as its financial year.

fixed asset *Accounting* Any property that is used in the production of goods and services, as buildings, machinery, etc. Any asset that cannot be readily converted to use other than that for which it was originally intended, in contrast to a current asset.

fixed charge *Accounting* Overhead that does not change regardless of whether anything is produced, such as rent or insurance.

fixed cost *Accounting* Any cost of production that does not change with quantity produced, as molds, setup charges, etc. Often used to describe the day to day cost of opening the doors and operating a business, as overhead.

fixed disk *Computers* A computer disk that is permanently mounted in its drive.

fixed overhead See *fixed charge*.

fixture *Accounting* Descriptive of any fitting or furniture, such as a light fixture, shelving, etc., that is affixed to a wall, ceiling, or floor in a building and that is considered thereby to be legally a part of the building.

flat *Accounting* Of that which is unchanged from one period to the next, as interest charges or an expense. *Marketing* Bought or sold at a set unit price regardless of volume.

flat rate *Marketing* A price that does not change with an increase in volume.

flex time Descriptive of a system whereby workers are given some latitude in selecting their hours of work. The intent of such a system is to relieve congestion on the roads going to and from work and to allow parents with young children to tailor their schedules to that of school or day care center.

float *Finance* The period between the time a check is drawn and the time it is actually charged to the maker's account.

floppy disk *Computers* A removable memory storage

device; a *diskette*.

floppy disk controller *Computers* The hardware and software that manages the operation of a disk drive.

flow chart A graphic illustration of the sequence of steps required to complete a task or series of tasks, as a manufacturing operation.

fluctuation Descriptive of frequent up and down movement, such as the price of materials or interest rates.

FOB or fob, free on board Designating delivery to a certain point by the seller without charge to the buyer. Terms of sale often specify *fob shipper's dock*, indicating that the freight is to be paid by the buyer, or *fob customer's dock*, in which case the seller pays the freight. The seller may choose to pay the freight and avoid liability for the shipment while in transit, by specifying *fob shipper, freight allowed to destination.*

font *Computers* Traditionally descriptive of one type face and style in one size. With the introduction of scalable fonts, one font often refers to a type face in a single style in a wide range of sizes.

font cartridge *Computers* A device that attaches to a printer to make additional fonts available to it.

Food and Drug Administration See *FDA*.

footnote *Finance* Information at the bottom of a financial statement that explains certain items in the report, such as for the effect of pending lawsuits, taxes, etc.

forecasting An attempt to predict future events based on available information. Forecasting future sales and production needs is the first step to budgeting for orderly growth of a company.

foreclosure *Law* The loss of right to a property as the result of failure to pay as agreed on a loan secured by the property.

foreign corporation A corporation organized in a foreign country or one that is conducting business in a state other than the one in which it is chartered.

foreground *Computer* Of processing that which takes place in the view of, and usually under the control of, the computer operator. Processing that has priority over all others.

foreman A man or woman who supervises the activities of a group of workers.

forfeiture *Law* The loss of property as a result of a violation of the law, or the failure to perform or exercise a right, such as for the loss of a deposit when the right to buy is not exercised.

forgery *Law* The illegal copying or counterfeiting of a document, signature, etc.

form *Computers* A document designed for the orderly entry of data; the configuration or arrangement of data in a report.

format Generally, a standard style, or layout, of data for a letter, report, etc. *Computers* The system that allows for the orderly storage and retrieval of data on a storage device as a disk. To initialize a disk to accept data. The system by which data is held in a particular file, such as spreadsheet or database. The layout, or arrangement, of information in a document.

form feed *Computers* A command to the printer to advance the paper the length of one form or one page.

formula

formula *Computers* A string of symbols that calculate to a value, as in a spreadsheet cell that calls for the total of the values in other specified cells, or that calculates to a logical *true* or *false* as in a conditional branch command.

FORTRAN, FORmula TRANslation *Computers* The first high level programmer's language to allow program statements using mathematical notation.

fortuitous Caused by accident or by chance, as of a loss covered by insurance or that may be deducted from taxable income.

forward *Commerce* To ship; to send on to another place.

forwarding company A company that specializes in the transfer of freight, as a consolidator that combines small shipments to fill a rail car, or one that overseas the movement of freight for export to a foreign country.

fragmentation *Computers* The condition of being broken into parts. A condition wherein files on a disk are recorded to scattered, rather than contiguous, segments.

frame *Computers* A window on a monitor screen that provides a view of information displayed by a program.

franchise *Law* Any special right granted by the government, such as for a business to operate as a corporation. The right to market a particular product or service, granted by the company that owns the rights to the brand or trade name.

fraud *Law* Deliberate deception to influence the surrender of something of value, as money, property, or rights, by another.

freedom of contract *Law* The right to enter into an agreement or covenant with others, that may only be restricted for the public good, such as for prohibition against an agreement that threatens the safety or welfare of another.

freedom of information *Law* Of federal legislation that provides the mechanism for making documents and materials of the government available to the general public.

free enterprise The concept of allowing business to operate in a competitive environment with a minimum of regulation by the government.

free market A business environment where pricing is driven by the laws of supply and demand without restraints of government, or any other unnatural force, such as a monopoly. The buying and selling of goods free from extraneous influence such as tariffs or quotas.

free on board See *fob*.

freight forwarder See *forwarding company*.

friction feed *Computers* A type of printer feed, usually used for single sheets.

fringe benefits *Labor Relations* Incentives offered by an organization to attract workers or negotiated by bargaining units for their members, comprising such things as sick pay, health insurance, paid vacations, and retirement plans.

front money *Finance* Advance payments, as a down payment, or funds to start an enterprise.

front office Generally, a reference to the offices of the upper management of a company, or the offices of the manager and support services in a particular plant as contrasted to those of line foremen or support services in the factory.

FTC See *Federal Trade Commission.*

fulfillment The processing of orders as they are received. Fulfillment may require merely sending an item of merchandise in return for the receipt of money or a promotional coupon. In other circumstances, such as for catalog or subscription sales, fulfillment requires the creation of a complete record of the transaction as well as selection and shipment of the items ordered.

full screen access *Computers* Descriptive of a program feature that allows editing of data anywhere on the computer monitor screen.

full service Descriptive of an organization, such as an advertising agency, a bank, a printer, etc. that purports to furnish a full range of related services in its field.

function code *Computers* Any symbol or set of symbols that generates an instruction to the computer.

function key *Computers* Where *n* equals a number, one of a set of ten or twelve keys that alone or in conjunction with Ctrl, Alt or Shift execute commands in certain programs.

FYI For your information.

gain *Accounting* The amount received for a property in excess of its book value.

gainful employment *Insurance* In a case of disability, an occupation suited to one who is disabled that provides earnings comparable to that pursued prior to the disabling injury or illness. *Law* An occupation that is suited to the abilities of the one employed.

garnishment *Law* A notice to an employer requiring that a portion of an employee's earnings be withheld for payment of a debt.

general contractor A person or company that enters into a contract for the construction, remodeling, etc. of a facility and accepts complete responsibility for materials, the work of sub contractors, etc.

general ledger *Accounting* A complete record of the accounts that make up the financial statements of a business. General ledger accounts are often a summary of detail from a subsidiary ledger, as *accounts receivable,* that represents the aggregate of all transactions from the accounts of individual customers.

general partner *Finance, Law* Any of the principals in a partnership whose liability for the debts of the firm is unlimited. See also *limited partnership*.

generic Generally, referring to an entire class or group. *Marketing* Descriptive of a product without a brand name.

GET *Computers* A program instruction to fetch data, a file or command from a non-contiguous source.

GIGO, garbage in garbage out *Computers* The axiom that the quality of information from computer processing is directly related to the quality of data entered into the computer.

glass ceiling *Colloq.* Descriptive of an invisible barrier in the ranks of a company's management above which women and minorities are not promoted.

global *Computers* Descriptive of formatting or instructions that affect all of the elements in a file or all of the files created by a program.

global search *Computers* Descriptive of a search through every directory, sub-directory or file on a disk; a command to find all occurrences of a string in a file, in a group of files or anywhere on the disk.

glut An excess; usually in reference to materials or finished goods that are available in quantities so much in excess of market demand that disposing of them will be difficult, even at reduced prices.

goal oriented A management style that is driven by the setting of specific goals and the formulating of detailed plans for reaching them.

go-between An intermediary. One who deals independently with each of two or more parties, often to clear the way for the establishment of an agreement between them.

going concern Of a company that is in operation, usually profitably. The value of a *going concern* is measured by its potential for profit in addition to the worth of its assets. *Accounting* The concept that financial transactions and records are based on the premise that the organization will continue in operation.

going private Descriptive of a business that is buying up its own stock or whose stock is being bought by a third party in sufficient quantity to eliminate a market in the stock.

going public The initial offering, for sale to the general public, of shares in a private company.

golden handcuffs Stock options, deferred bonuses, etc. that are part of the compensation package for a valuable employee, and that are forfeit if he or she leaves the company.

golden handshake Inducements offered to an employee to encourage early retirement.

golden parachute Part of the compensation package for a key executive of a firm targeted for takeover that provides for the payment of cash or other consideration if the executive is dismissed as a result of a takeover.

good faith Without malice or intent to deceive. *Labor Relations* Of the legal requirement that the parties representing labor and management meet to resolve disputes at a mutually agreeable time and place and with an open mind.

goods Generally, any moveable tangible property. *Manufacturing, Marketing* Merchandise that has been, or will be, produced for sale.

goodwill *Accounting* An intangible asset, the difference between the book value of a business and the price paid for that business, representing the value of established customers, reputation, etc.

GOTO *Computers* A program instruction to branch off to a new set of commands.

gouge To sell at a price that is excessive or well above fair market value.

graceful degradation *Computers* A decrease in performance of a computer that allows continued operation at a lower efficiency level or that allows an orderly shutdown without loss of data.

grace period Descriptive of a contract provision that allows additional time for renewal at the end of the contract, as of a loan or insurance policy.

graduated wage *Labor Relations* A pay scale that

provides for adjustment based on length of service, quality or quantity of output, etc.

grammar checker *Computers* A program that inspects a file or document for grammatical errors, advises the user of the error and suggests alternatives.

grandfather clause *Law* A provision in a new regulation or legislation that exempts those already engaged in the activity being regulated.

grapevine *Colloq.* The rumor mill; the unofficial lines of communication within an organization.

graph *Computers* A chart that displays the relative magnitude of associated elements as bars, columns, or sections of a pie.

graphic display *Computers* The depiction of graphic elements on a computer monitor screen.

graphics capability *Computers* A computer monitor with a graphic interface that permits the depiction of picture elements on screen; a printer that has the ability to print picture elements.

gratis Free; offered without charge or other consideration.

gratuitous Given without having been requested.

grid *Computers* A pattern of columns and rows for recording data as for a spreadsheet or for positioning elements as for optical character recognition.

grievance procedure *Labor Relations* The formal process by which a worker may air a complaint against an employer or a union.

gross *Finance, Manufacturing* The total amount before adjustments, as for taxes, damaged goods, etc.

group dynamics The study of the interpersonal relationships between the members of a work group.

growth rate A comparison of change during a number of like periods for some aspect of a company, as number of employees, units produced, sales, equity, etc.

guarantee *Marketing* An assurance that an item will be repaired or replaced if it does not meet with the approval of the buyer.

guaranteed annual wage A minimum assured earnings level for certain hourly workers in a company. Such assurance is normally part of an agreement that the worker will accept overtime work or transfer to other jobs as required by production demands.

guild A medieval union, formed for the mutual protection of those engaged in a particular trade or craft. Occasionally used today to designate a union whose members are employed at a craft, as a *bookbinder's guild* or an *artist's guild*.

hacker *Computers* One who has acquired skill in the use of computers for personal pleasure.

halt *Computers* The untimely termination of computer processing.

hand held computer *Computers* A computer small enough to be held in the hand, often used to keep track of appointments and addresses.

handling Generally, the act and cost of moving materials or products in a manufacturing plant, placing items in inventory, removing and packing them for shipping, etc. Often, a charge for services not included in a quoted price, such as for storage and retrieval, or drop shipping of merchandise. Such a charge is often incurred when a buyer places a large custom order that is to be shipped to several destinations or at different times and the exact shipping information is not known at the time the order is placed; the seller then prices the item to be manufactured and both parties agree that additional handling costs will be billed as they are incurred. Occasionally, the term is used to describe the cost of buying on credit.

handshaking *Computers* The protocol for identification and communication between two pieces of equipment.

hang-up *Computers* A temporary halt in processing.

hard copy Descriptive of a source or substantiating document that is the basis for data entry, such as an accounting transaction, or authorization for an action, such as entry of an order. *Computers* A printout of data.

hard currency *Finance* A medium of exchange that is recognized throughout the world as relatively stable.

hard disk *Computers* A disk that is mounted with its own drive, usually installed in the computer case.

hard error *Computers* An equipment malfunction or mistake in processing caused by hardware.

hard goods *Marketing* Durable property. Normally, a reference to consumer assets with a life expectancy greater than one year, as furniture, major appliances, etc.

hard sell *Marketing* A direct sales or advertising technique that stresses the importance of buying, or agreeing to buy, immediately, often by implying that dire consequences may be the result of delay. See also *soft sell.*

hardware *Computers* The computer itself and any of

the peripheral devices that are a part of the system.

Hawthorne effect The inclination of an individuals to knowingly or unknowingly alter their behavior under certain circumstances, such as when they are being monitored, or when acting in a changed set of circumstances; an important factor for consideration when doing time studies or monitoring any activity.

Hawthorne studies An extensive study of the workers at the Western Electric Company's Hawthorne plant in Cicero, Illinois, that attempted to relate a variety of elements in the workplace to improved productivity and worker satisfaction.

head *Computers* The read/write head in a disk drive. The device on an impact or ink jet printer that transfers characters to paper.

head crash *Computers* A circumstance in which the read/write head contacts the surface of the disk.

header *Computers* A headline on a document or report.

headhunter *Colloq.* A firm or the representative of a firm that specializes in placing key personnel, such as managers or sales representatives. Unlike most employment agencies that work for and collect a fee from the prospective employee, the headhunter works for and collects fees from the prospective employer. Most successful headhunters specialize, or are part of an organization that has separate divisions that specialize, in a particular industry or type of job.

health maintenance organization See *HMO*.

hearing A formal meeting before a judge, referee, company executive, appointed committee, etc., at which interested parties present evidence or testimony regarding the matter at hand. The purpose of the hearing may be for the party or parties conducting the hearing to enter a judgment, to recommend action, or simply to gather information for further consideration.

hearsay Something one has heard, but cannot confirm as true.

hearsay evidence *Law* Testimony that relates to something heard by a witness, but not actually observed or experienced by that witness.

hedging The avoidance of total commitment. Modifying a statement to avoid taking an uncompromising position. *Commerce* Any action taken to protect ones position, as placing a tentative order for vital materials in anticipation of need, or as protection against the failure of a primary supplier to deliver. *Finance* Any arrangement to protect cash flow, as by a line of credit to offset possible cost overruns or failure of a client to pay on time.

Help *Computers* A feature in most programs that offers guidance to the user; see also context sensitive help.

help screen *Computers* On screen guidance for the user, often interactive, allowing a selection of subjects about which the program offers information.

heuristic Learning by applying what is known toward solving a problem, recording the results, and using that which has been learned in the next step toward a solution. Problem-solving by the use of trial and error, in contrast to an algorithm.

hexadecimal *Computers* A numbering system in base

sixteen used in computer notation.

hidden agenda Objectives of an individual or group that are not readily apparent. Often applied in the negative sense, as for one who critiques the work of another on the pretext of being helpful, but who really is striving to discredit the other.

hidden tax A tax that is built into the cost of an item and so not apparent to the buyer.

hierarchical Of any structural order that branches directly from the point of greatest importance through various levels of a lower order, as the organization chart of a business that proceeds from the chief executive or general manager to those on a secondary level who report to him or her, with further branches indicating those who report to second-level executives, and so on. *Computers* Of the directory structure that has as its entry point the *boot directory* containing the basic files and instructions that allow the operator to access other directories containing commands, programs, data, etc. The boot directory is *parent directory* to those at the second level, that may, in turn, hold files and be parent to directories at the next level, etc.

high level language *Computes* A programming language that is somewhat similar to spoken language.

highlighted *Computes* An element on the screen that is set apart from others by underlining, reverse video or contrasting color; of a block of copy or graphic element that has been selected for some purpose.

historical cost *Accounting* The cost of purchase or acquisition; reference to the accounting principle that requires the reporting of assets at their original cost on financial statements.

hit list *Colloq.* Those persons or things that are the target of some action. Often used in the negative sense, as a list of employees to be dismissed, the hit list may also be positive, as denoting objectives to be aggressively pursued. Such a list may be one of target accounts for sales, problems to be corrected, etc.

HMO, health maintenance organization A health insurance plan whereby a company contracts to furnish medical care to a group of workers through medical personnel and organizations with whom it has contracted for such services.

holdback Generally, of money not paid until certain conditions are met. *Accounting, Commerce* Part of an invoice that is not paid until goods have been inspected and found acceptable. *Labor* A portion of wages held be the employer as security for the return of tools, uniforms, etc. supplied to a worker. That portion of wages that is in arrears throughout the length of employment as a result of the time lag between reporting and preparing the payroll.

holding company A corporation whose only asset is the stock of a subsidiary company or companies. The holding company is usually actively involved in overseeing the management of the companies it controls, and is often instrumental in initiating inter company activities.

home based business An enterprise for profit operated from a private dwelling that also serves as a residence. In some cases work is performed in the home, such as one that produces handicrafts or repairs small appliances; in others, the work is performed outside, as for painting, plumbing, carpentry, etc.

Home key *Computers* A cursor movement key that sends the cursor to the beginning of a line of text and, used in conjunction with other keys, to the top left of the screen, the top of the page or the beginning of a file.

honor *Accounting* To accept as correct, as an invoice. *Commerce* To accept and carry out an obligation, as of a contract. *Finance* To pay when due, as of a legal debt.

honorarium A payment for services for which no fee has been set and for which there is no legal obligation, as to a public speaker.

horizontal integration Expansion of a company in its main field of endeavor or a closely allied field at the same stage of production, often through the absorption of another company. A manufacturer of wood furniture, for example, may buy out another manufacturer of furniture, or a supplier of metal brackets or cushions used in the manufacturing process. See also *vertical integration*.

hot key *Computers* A key combination that executes a macro or command that would otherwise require several key strokes.

hot line *Computers* A telephone number provided by an equipment or software manufacturer or dealer through which a user may access technical help.

house brand See *private brand*.

housekeeping *Computers* The process of deleting old files, arranging files in their proper directories and maintaining an orderly file structure for efficient operation.

housing code Of local ordinance that pertains to the maintenance of standards for safety, sanitation, etc. required for residential occupancy of a dwelling. See also *building code*.

huckster Generally, a street peddler. *Marketing* One who promotes a product, especially through mass media. *Colloq.* Often, of a salesperson whose presentation and tactics are questionable; one who lacks credibility.

human relations The study of the importance of the individual in the success of an enterprise and the interaction of personnel in the workplace. Descriptive of efforts to motivate individuals by recognition of their importance and involvement in the organization.

human resources The function of managing personnel in an organization, with responsibility for hiring, training, administration of benefit programs, maintaining records, etc.

hype *Colloq.* Often describing excessive, and perhaps unwarranted, claims. *Marketing* Extensive promotion to attract consumer interest.

hypothesis A supposition established as a basis for further investigation or discussion.

ICC, Interstate Commerce Commission A federal agency established in 1887 to regulate the rates and service of carriers engaged in interstate commerce.

icon *Computers* A graphic image on a monitor screen that represents a directory, file, utility, etc. and that can be selected with a mouse click.

ideal capacity The maximum output possible under

theoretical conditions in which a machine or plant operates continuously with no delays or down time.

idle time *Manufacturing* A period during which there is no output of value, because of equipment malfunction, lack of materials, lack of scheduled work, etc.

IF statement *Computers* A select word in a conditional branch specifying that IF a condition exists, the first set of instructions is to be followed, otherwise, follow a different set of instructions.

illegal character *Computers* A symbol that is unacceptable in a specific situation, as those symbols not available in a particular type font or a letter placed in a database number field.

illegal instruction *Computers* A reserved word or command in a formula that is not available in that particular program.

illegal strike *Labor Relations* A strike that is in violation of the law, that has not been voted and authorized by established procedure, or that is in violation of a legal contract.

image *Marketing* The way in which a product is viewed by those in its target market or by the general public. The impression that is intended to be created by advertising or publicity.

image enhancement *Computers* Altering or improving a graphic image such as art or a photograph by use of a computer program.

imaging *Computers* To create or modify a graphic representation with the use of a computer.

impact printer *Computers* A printer that creates an image by striking the paper.

impasse Generally, a deadlock; a disagreement that cannot be resolved. *Labor Relations* In negotiations, a point on which neither side is willing to give ground, making compromise impossible.

implementation To put into practice, or carry out, as a plan.

implied Not clearly expressed; suggested, often by circumstance. *Law* That which is not clearly expressed, but that may be inferred by a reasonable person under normal circumstances.

import *Commerce* To bring into the country, often for sale, goods produced in another country. The product so imported.

import quota *Commerce* A restriction on the amount of certain goods that can be brought into the country and offered for sale, normally to protect the jobs of those in the importing country producing similar goods.

imposition That which is exacted, as a tax, or toll. *Labor Relations* The placing of an unjust burden or demand, as short notice of a requirement to work overtime. Many labor contracts place restrictions on such demands, allowing for refusal without penalty.

impound To take into custody and hold property, funds, etc. pending resolution of a legal matter, as an overdue debt.

imprint Generally, to mark in some way. *Commerce* The name of a company, or a company brand, set in a particular type face or design, often with graphic embellishment; a company logo; in effect, the company's signature. Information on the outside of a shipping carton that describes the contents, quantity, etc. *Manufacturing* To mark parts with the manufacturer's or distributor's brand by stamping, printing, etc.

improvement *Accounting* Any change in equipment, building, property, etc. that increases its book value.

impulse merchandise *Marketing* Goods likely to be bought on a whim. Such goods are most effectively sold in heavy traffic areas or near the checkout counters in a store.

imputed cost *Accounting* An expense that may be ascribed, though not actually incurred, such as the interest that would be charged if materials in inventory were purchased on credit.

imputed liability See *vicarious liability*.

inadvertent Unintentional; descriptive of that caused by oversight, usually without fixing blame.

incapacity Generally, disability or lack of fitness. *Law* Not qualified, as to enter into a contract by reason of age, mental incompetence, etc.

incentive That proffered to encourage or motivate as *incentive pay* for greater production. *Marketing* A premium, special price, etc. to encourage the purchase of a product.

incidental Of that which is secondary, or associated with something of greater importance, as *incidental income* from the sale of waste.

inclusive *Computers* Incorporating as part of the whole, such as the part of a formula in which terms or values joined by the reserved word *AND,* often enclosed by parenthesis, must both be considered in evaluating the formula.

income *Accounting* Monies received for the sale of

goods or services that is the primary business of a company, or from incidental sources.

income account The ledger accounts that relate to profit and loss, including all revenue and expense accounts.

income property Property that is held for the purpose of producing revenue by rental, capital gains, or both.

income statement The financial statement that summarizes revenue, expenses, depreciation, etc. to show the income or loss from operations.

incompetent Descriptive of one who is incapable of performing his or her job properly. *Law* One who is not legally capable of entering into a contract by reason of mental deficiency.

incorporate To join to something that already exists, or to merge diverse elements into a unified whole. *Law* To form a business into a corporation according to the laws of a particular state.

incremental increase *Labor* A periodic increase in wages or salary according to a set scale based on time on the job. *Marketing* A periodic increase in selling price over the term of a contract to cover anticipated additions to the cost of labor and materials.

indemnity *Insurance* Protection against losses through an insurance contract. Payment for a claim of losses covered by insurance. *Law* Legal immunity from liability by certain parties or for certain actions.

independent adjuster A claims adjuster who operates as an independent contractor for one or more insurance companies.

independent audit *Accounting* Review of a company's

financial records by an accounting firm that is not affiliated in any other way with the company. It is expected that the auditor from such a company can render an unbiased opinion as to whether the company is maintaining its records according to generally accepted accounting principles.

independent contractor One who performs work for a company, and is paid as a vendor rather than an employee. Tax law sets forth a number of criteria that must be met for a worker to be considered an independent contractor: the employer cannot set hours of work, place of work, furnish a significant portion of tools to perform the job, directly supervise the work in progress, etc. The independent contractor is paid in full with no deductions for withholding or FICA; he or she is responsible for filing an estimated tax form and paying self-employment tax.

indexing *Labor Relations* Adjusting wages based on an index, such as the Consumer Price Index.

indirect cost *Accounting* Any expense for labor, materials, overhead, etc. that is not related directly to the manufacture of the product, group of products, or service that a company offers for sale.

indirect labor *Accounting* The cost of labor that is not related directly to the manufacture of the product, group of products, or service that a company offers for sale.

indirect overhead *Accounting* Any overhead expense that is not related to the manufacturing operation, as the salaries of front office personnel, the cost of office space or office supplies.

inductive reasoning A problem solving technique

that draws on limited information to form a more general conclusion.

industrial advertising Promotion directed to other businesses rather than the end user, as for the sale of materials, supplies, or services required for the production of other goods or services.

industrial engineering The study and implementation of the most effective integration of the tools of production—personnel, materials, and equipment.

industrial park An area designed for occupancy by companies engaged in manufacturing and those who service such companies, such as trucking or industrial supply companies.

industrial psychology The study of behavior and motivation in the workplace. The industrial psychologist offers assistance in such areas as the selection, training and promotion processes; analyzing tasks; and the measurement and improvement of performance.

industrial relations Descriptive of the interaction between supervisors and the employees who report to them in a company. Often used to describe the relationship between the management of a company and a union.

industry Any extensive business activity, often referring to all those in a similar business, as the *housing industry* or the *automotive industry*.

industry standard Specifications that tend to be relatively uniform throughout all areas of business, such as electrical outlets, computer couplers, automobile tires, clothing sizes, etc. Such standards may be set by law or regulation of a government agency, by an independent organization such as the American National Standards Institute, or by tacit agreement among manufacturers. Industry standards may be set to establish minimum safety requirements or to offer compatibility between different brands of the same items.

inelasticity Generally, the characteristic of being inflexible or not easily adaptable. *Marketing* The condition of unvarying demand, that is, a product for which demand does not increase appreciably when the price is lowered, nor does demand fall off when the price is increased.

inflation A general increase in price levels, particularly of necessities, that decreases the purchasing power of a dollar.

inflation rate The rate of increase in price levels expressed as a percentage of increase or a ratio between price levels at two distinct times, often measured monthly and expressed as an annual rate.

influence The power to affect others. Have an effect on the actions or behavior of another. *Accounting* Often an expression of the relationship between ledger accounts, that is, the way in which a change in one account affects the value of others. *Marketing* Any attempt through advertising or promotion to alter or mold the behavior of the buyer. Of an individual, circumstance, etc. that does not directly initiate a purchase, but that does significantly influence the purchaser.

information Any knowledge, data, or fact. *Computers* any data that can be stored, retrieved and manipulated by a computer.

information management *Computers* The systems and techniques involved in effectively compiling and manipulating useful data.

information processing *Computers* The manipulation of compiled data and the compilation of reports from the data.

information retrieval *Computers* Descriptive of the techniques for accessing data from storage in the form or pattern that the user desires.

infringement *Law* Any violation, disregard or breech of the rights of another, especially concerning rights at law, as of a contract, patent, copyright, etc.

in-house services Generally, of a department or departments in a company providing services peripheral to the operation of the business, that are normally supplied by outside vendors, such as an *in-house printing plant, art department, advertising agency,* etc. Such undertakings are not a part of the products or services offered for sale by a company, but may be taken on when there is no vendor who can meet the special needs of the company, or when it is determined that the tasks can be performed more economically in house.

initialize *Computers* To format a disk to accept data; to boot up a computer by loading the system files it needs to become functional.

initiative The tendency to think and take action on one's own, without instructions from another.

injunction *Law* An order by a court, to a person or organization, prohibiting an action or directing that a course of action to be stopped.

in kind Generally, the exchange or replacement of

property with material that is comparable in quality and value. Also, of services that are to be performed in a like or similar fashion.

ink jet *Computers* Of a high-quality printer that forms images on paper or other material by squirting minuscule jets of ink in patterns determined by the computer.

innovation Of the introduction of new ideas or concepts.

innovation strategy The management concept that constantly looks to new technology, methods, etc. for improvements in product, service, or performance.

in-pack *Marketing* Of a premium that is included in the package with the product, such as a toy or small book in a box of cereal. See also *on-pack*.

input Generally, anything that is put in, as an investment in an enterprise, or new information and ideas brought into a discussion. *Computers* Any information conveyed to a computer or peripheral from the keyboard, a disk or other memory device, or an external source, such as a telephone line for storage or processing.

input buffer *Computers* The area of computer memory that accepts and stores input for transfer to its destination.

input device *Computers* Any equipment linked to the computer that enters source data, such as a keyboard, an optical scanner or a modem.

input/output, I/O *Computers* A reference to the conventions for transmitting data between a computer and its peripherals or an external device.

inside information *Financial* Information that has

not been made public, available only to an insider, and that may impact on the value of an investment, as by an offer for a takeover, or a dramatic change in company finances or prospects. Securities and exchange commission rules forbid trading on the basis of such information.

insider *Financial* One who by reason of his or her position has access to information about a company or investment that is not available to the stockholders or to the general public.

insider trading *Financial* Illegal trading in a stock based on insider information.

insolvency *Financial* The condition of being unable to meet ones debts; bankruptcy.

inspection Generally, a careful examination. *Manufacturing* Examination of materials as they are received to confirm that they meet required specifications. Examination of a product at various stages of production to confirm that a certain standard of quality is being maintained. Such inspection may be the ongoing responsibility of personnel on an assembly line, or it may be that of independent quality control personnel. See also *quality control*.

installation *Computers* The process of setting up and configuring a computer system or program; the computer system so installed.

installment contract Generally, any agreement that calls for periodic performance at regular intervals, as the payment of debt, shipment of merchandise, providing of a service, etc. *Finance* A credit arrangement whereby interest for the period of a contract is calculated on and combined with: the cost of goods purchased, state and local sales taxes, delivery charges, etc., less any down payment; the total is then divided into equal payments, or installments, to be paid over the life of the agreement. Most automobiles are purchased on an installment contract.

institution A firmly entrenched tradition or practice. A public organization, as a corporation, bank, library, hospital, etc.

institutional advertising Of the promotion of an organization's image in contrast to the selling of a product. Such promotion may stress a concern for quality, community involvement, or the part a company plays in contributing to goods and services furnished by others. Institutional advertising has been found to be an employee morale booster in communities where the organization maintains a facility for supplying goods and services that are not readily identifiable in the final product.

instruction *Computers* A direction to the computer to set a parameter or execute an operation.

instruction code *Computers* The language understood by a particular computer or program.

instruction format *Computers* The syntax required by a particular program for issuing a command.

insurability *Insurance* Of that which may or may not be insured; of the qualities that determine whether a thing may be insured. Insurability of an employee under a company's life or medical plan, for example, may be limited for a new employee past a certain age. Insurability of a structure against certain hazards may be limited, as well, by the age of the building or its location.

insurable interest *Insurance* An expression of the interest of the policy holder in the unaltered continuance of the existence of the insured. One may only have an insurable interest if benefit is derived from the existence of the person or property insured and such benefit would be terminated if the insured ceased to exist. Life insurance on an individual, for example, may be protection to insure repayment of a debt, or to indemnify one for loss of affection. Insurance against property loss may cover indemnification for the loss of the use of the property, for the cost of replacement, or to provide income that would have been enjoyed if the property had continued in existence.

insurance A system of protection against losses that provides for payments by those who seek such protection to those who agree to provide compensation in the event of a loss. Such losses are clearly specified in a contract as to type and amount of compensation. Payments for protection, or premiums, are based on the amount of coverage and risk factors, such as the age of an individual in the case of life insurance, or type of structure in the case of insurance on a structure.

insured Covered by insurance. Of a person or property that is protected by insurance. Of the policy holder; one who is protected from loss. *Colloq.* Of that which is virtually certain; assured.

insured mail A type of protection offered by the postal service in which the sender is compensated to the extent of the declared value of the contents of a letter or package that is lost or damaged in transit.

insurer The person or company that, for a fee, agrees to protect another against a monetary loss.

intangible asset *Accounting* Descriptive of items on the company books that have value, but are without substance, such as goodwill, trademarks, copyrights, patents, etc.

integrated circuit *Computers* An electronic device that is comprised of a number of connected circuit elements formed on a single chip of semiconductor material; a microprocessor.

integrated software *Computers* A package that combines several functions in a single program, such as one that features word processing, spreadsheet, and a database manager. Word processing and spreadsheet programs often contain a graphics program that makes it possible to add charts or artwork to enhance the visual impact of reports.

integrated system *Computers* A combination of computers, programs, and peripherals that are designed to work together.

integration The bringing together or blending of otherwise disparate elements. The merging of the operation of two companies, divisions or departments, often under a single manager.

integrity The quality of being sound or complete, as the *integrity* of information. Honesty or high moral standards, as shown in business dealings.

interactive processing, interactive program *Computers* Processing of data that takes place as commands are entered by the operator. Once processing is completed, the computer waits for a new command, as contrasted to **batch processing.**

interest *Finance* A share or claim in a venture, usually expressed as a portion or percentage of the total investment. The cost of borrowing, usually expressed as a flat amount or an annual percentage of the outstanding balance of a loan.

interface *Computers* Hardware or software that forms a link between devices and allows them to communicate with each other.

interim audit *Finance* A review of a company's financial records for a period that is not the end of the fiscal year. Such an audit may be conducted prior to the issuing of an interim statement, or in anticipation of the annual audit.

interim statement *Finance* A financial report that covers a part of the year, such as a quarterly report. Such reports often lack the detail and precision of the annual report, but serve primarily as a means to keep shareholders apprised of company activities and performance.

interleaving *Computers* A routine that directs the computer to switch between applications, thus appearing to run both at the same time, such as printing in the background while accepting new data entered in the foreground.

interlocking directorates Descriptive of two or more companies that have one or more members of their board of directors in common.

interlocutory *Law* A decision handed down during the course of a court action, pending final disposition of the suit.

intermediary Generally, one who serves as an emissary or arbitrator, as a head hunter or mediator.

intermittent processing *Manufacturing* Descriptive of a type of operation that involves the production of a variety of goods, such as a print shop where once the required quantity of an item is produced, the equipment is shut down to be prepared for the production of a fixed quantity of the next item. See also *continuous processing*.

internal audit *Accounting* A review of a company's financial records and the system for maintaining them by an individual appointed for that purpose from within the company. The internal audit may be to seek out the cause of discrepancies in accounts, or simply to confirm that standard policy and procedure as set by management are being followed. *Manufacturing* A review of operations by an individual or group from within the company to assess the effectiveness of systems and to recommend how they might be improved.

internal storage *Computers* Memory for the storage of data that is built into, and directly accessible by, the computer.

internship A training, or introductory period for a new, usually young, executive, during which time the subject may be exposed to a number of different jobs in various departments in order to become familiar with the company.

interrupt *Computers* A control signal that directs the computer to halt processing on one level and move to another.

interrupt priority *Computers* The order of precedence in which signals are processed, for example, input from the keyboard usually has priority over background printing.

Interstate Commerce Commission See *ICC*.

in the black *Colloq.* Descriptive of a business, department, product, etc. that is showing a profit.

in the red *Colloq.* Descriptive of a business, department, product, etc. that is showing a loss.

in transit *Commerce* Descriptive of goods that are out of the hands of the shipper and on the way to their destination.

inventory *Accounting* An asset comprised of all materials, supplies, finished goods or goods in some stage of processing that are owned by a company, whether located physically on the premises of that company, in transit, or in the hands of a distributor who has them on consignment.

inventory control The system by which inventory is managed. The recording of goods as they are received and as they are dispersed, so that an inventory balance may be maintained and periodically checked against a physical count.

inventory turnover The frequency with which the usual order quantity of an item, or items, is dispensed over a given period; one of the factors used to determine the optimum order quantity. A comparison of the cost of goods sold during an accounting period with the average cost of inventory, which may be expressed as the number of times that inventory is replaced during the period or the average length of time that goods are held in inventory.

invoice *Accounting* A bill; a detailed list of charges for goods or services that is sent to the purchaser.

involuntary conversion Condemnation; the taking of

private property for public use. See also *just compensation.*

irregular A product with a cosmetic fault that does not impair function, such as an appliance with blistered paint or clothing with a pull in the fabric; such items are often sold through special outlets as seconds.

iteration A repetition. *Computers* A programming technique that causes an operation to be repeated until a certain condition is met, as in a search of a database file where successive lines are read until a match is found or the end of the file is reached.

itinerant worker A laborer who moves from place to place to find temporary employment, often a farm worker.

job A particular type of work, as a trade or vocation; see also job description. A position or place of employment. A specific task or set of tasks that, taken together, achieve a particular purpose, as *the job of mowing the lawn. Manufacturing* A production unit that comprises all of the goods produced to fill a specific order for a client; see also job order.

job action *Labor Relations* A demonstration by employees to press for the acceptance of certain demands, often by refusing to work overtime, or by strict adherence to work rules that causes a slowing down of production.

jobber *Commerce* One who buys goods from a manufacturer or importer for resale to a dealer or merchant. *Manufacturing* A company that produces goods to order, each production lot covered by a job order. See also *job shop.*

job classification An ordering of jobs in a company or industry that takes into account the level of knowledge and skill required for the job so as to group like jobs and establish a wage range for each group.

job cost *Accounting* All of the expense for labor, materials, and overhead, tracked by recording workers' time, materials invoices, etc., that is attributable to a particular job order for a client.

job description *Labor Relations* A detailed definition of a specific position or type of work within a company or an industry, including education and experience required, duties and responsibilities of the person filling the position, etc.

job entry *Manufacturing* All of the related tasks necessary to place work into production, such as by confirming prices and specifications, creating a job jacket, requisitioning materials, confirming production schedules, setting up a file to record costs, etc.

job jacket *Manufacturing* A specification sheet that identifies a particular job order and contains such information as the name of the client, goods to be produced, quantity to be produced, materials required, delivery date, etc., often printed on, or attached to, an envelope or folder to hold drawings, notes, samples, etc. Also called a *job ticket*.

job lot *Commerce* An assortment of merchandise, often of textiles, containing a variety of colors, sizes, styles, etc. Frequently used in reference to irregulars.

job order *Manufacturing* Authorization to produce a set quantity of a particular product for a specific customer. The merchandise so authorized.

job placement The process of matching individuals to jobs for which they are suited. The processing may take place within a company, by the personnel or human resources department, or within an industry or labor market by an employment agency.

job processing *Accounting* A cost accounting system in which items are manufactured in a job lot of a particular size or quantity and costs are accumulated for each job. See also **batch processing**. *Computers* The execution of a task or series of tasks for processing data.

job shop *Manufacturing* Descriptive of a company that operates on a job order system, that is, all work done must be authorized by a **job order** containing all of the necessary information about the goods to be manufactured or the services to be performed.

job ticket See **job jacket**.

joint account *Finance* Of a bank or brokerage account set up by two or more persons. Such an account may be set up to allow any one of the participants to authorize a transaction, or the signature of all may be required.

joint liability *Law* Of those relationships in which there is a shared responsibility for the payment of a debt or other obligation.

jointly and severally *Law* A type of joint liability in which the parties to a contract may be held accountable as a group, or separately as individuals, that is, each member has unlimited liability up to the total outstanding amount of the obligation.

joint tenancy *Law* Ownership of property by two or

more persons, with ownership passing to the survivor or survivors in the event of the death of one of the owners. Also called *joint tenancy with the right of survivorship, joint tenants but not tenants in common,* etc. depending on the requirements of the laws of the state in which the agreement is drawn. See also *tenancy in common.*

joint venture An agreement by two or more individuals or companies to join forces and share responsibility for a project that could not be accomplished singly. Such an agreement is normally for the duration of a single project and ends when the project is completed. Also, the project undertaken.

journal Generally, a record of information and events, as recorded by an individual, or in a publication for those engaged in a scientific, academic or professional field of endeavor. *Accounting* The original record of transactions that are summarized to report the financial activities and changes in a company.

journal entry, journalize *Accounting* The recording, in a journal, of the financial transactions of a company.

journeyman A skilled worker who has completed the apprenticeship required for recognition and acceptance as a proficient craftsman.

judgment lien *Law* A court order that allows a creditor to lay claim to property in order to satisfy a debt.

junior partner A partner with a subordinate interest in a firm; one who plays a limited role in the management of the company and is eligible for a limited share of profits.

junk bond *Finance* A bond that pays a high yield to compensate for a relatively higher risk factor.

just compensation *Law* Reasonable damages paid to one who sustains a loss as the result of an involuntary conversion.

justifiable That which can be shown to be reasonable. *Law* Of an act, or failure to act, that can be excused by reason of an action, or lack of action, on the part of another, as the withholding of payment when merchandise is not delivered.

justification *Accounting* A report that defends or advocates an expenditure, such as for a new machine, and that points out benefits of increased production or reduced cost, how the acquisition is to be financed, etc. *Computers* In word processing, the spacing of text so that it is lined up at both side margins; also called *full justification.*

kerning *Computers* In word processing or desktop publishing, descriptive of proportional spacing between typeset characters.

keyboard *Computers* A panel of buttons containing the alphabet, numbers and various symbols used as the primary device for entering data into a computer.

keyboard lockout *Computers* A program feature that prevents further entry from the keyboard while the computer is processing. A security device to prevent access to the computer by unauthorized users

keypad *Computers* A small, special purpose keyboard with a limited number of buttons.

key person insurance Protection against the loss of the services of a principle in a business. Such protection may seek to compensate survivors for the reduction in the value of their investment when the services of the insured are lost, or it may be to provide cash flow to keep the business operating during an adjustment period.

keying The practice of linking a variable to a standard, such as linking a wage or price increase in a contract to the Consumer Price Index. *Marketing* Coding that is printed on a coupon in a flyer, mailer, or space advertisement in order to link the response to the source.

key word *Computers* A word or set of words in a program or formula that indicate the operation to be performed.

kickback An illegal payment to an individual for approving a purchase, contract, etc. *Labor Relations* An illegal payment demanded of an employee by an employer or union in return for job security.

kicker *Colloq.* An added incentive, as a premium offered with the purchase of a consumer product, or special services or credit terms offered in conjunction with an industrial contract.

kill *Colloq.* Generally, to end or terminate, as a project or proposal.

killing *Colloq.* Descriptive of an abnormally high profit on a transaction.

kilobyte, KB *Computers* One thousand bytes.

kiting *Finance* To alternately write and deposit checks between two or more bank accounts, taking advantage of the *float.* The alteration of a check illegally to increase its face value.

kudos Recognition or praise for a job well done.

labeling requirements Federal and state regulations

that require warning labels on containers of poisons and other hazardous substances.

labor Work; the physical effort required to accomplish a task. Those who work for wages, in contrast to *management*. A reference to labor unions collectively.

labor agreement The terms and conditions of a contract between labor and management. The contract so joined.

labor dispute A disagreement between labor and management that may arise in the course of negotiating a contract or in the interpretation of a contract.

labor force Collectively, the workers on a job; those employed by a company; or those of the nation, defined by age, who are employed or seeking employment.

labor intensive Descriptive of a business, industry, product, or service in which the cost of production is largely for workers, that is, the production of goods or services that do not lend themselves to automation. See also *capital intensive*.

labor relations See *industrial relations*.

labor union An organization authorized to negotiate pay scales, fringe benefits, working conditions, etc. with an employer as the sole representative of a group of workers comprising a bargaining unit.

laissez-faire *French* The concept that business should be allowed to operate with a minimum of government control or regulation.

LAN, local area network *Computers* A group of computers that are linked to share common programs, data, output devices, etc.

land Real property that can be conveyed by deed.

land locked A section of real property that does not have direct access to a public thoroughfare, and must be reached by an easement through adjacent land.

landlord One who owns land that is leased to others.

landmark Generally, a marker that fixes the boundary of land or a prominent feature that serves to identify a locality. *Law* A ruling that establishes an important precedent.

land-office business *Colloq.* Descriptive of a very busy trade.

language *Computers* A precise system of vocabulary and syntax for writing programs; *absolute* or *machine* language refers to instructions that can be understood directly by the computer; an *artificial* or *high level* language more closely emulates spoken English to make programming easier.

lapse *Insurance* The termination of a policy for failure to pay the premium. *Law* The termination or loss of a right because of some contingency, as a loss of property through failure to maintain or pay taxes.

laptop computer

laptop computer *Computer* A small computer with built-in monitor and keyboard that is between a **desktop computer** and a **notebook computer** in size. See also **microcomputer**.

laser, Light Amplification by Stimulated Emission of Radiation *Computers* A device that emits intense light of a precise wavelength.

laser disk *Computers* A storage disk that is read using laser technology.

laser printer *Computers* An electrostatic printer that creates a high quality image with the use of laser technology..

last in, first out See *LIFO*.

law Generally, the rules of conduct láid down and enforced by governing authority. The study of the rules of conduct established by legislation and by custom or tradition.

law of supply and demand The theory that in a free market, the relationship between supply and demand will directly affect price and the quantity available at that price.

layoff *Labor* The removal of an employee from the payroll, usually temporary, during a time of reduced demand.

lcl or **LCL, less than carload** A classification for shipments that are too small to require a full rail car and are to be held for combining with other small shipments going in the same direction before a car can be dispatched.

LCD, liquid crystal display *Computers* a monitor screen that uses liquid crystals to create an image.

lead time Generally, the lapsed time required for a sequence of events. *Manufacturing* The time required for delivery of a product, from the placing of the order to shipping. *Marketing* The time required to plan and implement an advertising campaign, from conception to placement of the advertising. The time between insertion of a print ad and the print date. The time required to bring a new product to market, from concept to distribution.

leasehold improvement *Accounting* Enhancement of

leased property, as by constructing offices or production areas, installing lighting, etc. Once attached to the property, the improvements are considered part of the property and cannot be removed except for further improvement; however, the cost of labor and fixtures may be entered on the books as an asset and depreciated.

leave of absence *Labor Relations* A time away from work, usually for an extended period without pay. A leave of absence presumes a return to the same or a comparable position at the end of the leave. An individual may take leave, for example, to serve for a time as a political appointee.

ledger *Accounting* The book of final entry for accounting transactions, summarized from journal entries and forming the data that makes up the financial reports of an organization.

legal entity *Law* An individual or organization that is recognized as being able to enter into a contract and that may be sued for failure to perform.

legal right *Law* Any privilege, interest or claim that is protected by law.

legal tender *Law* Money that may be offered to satisfy a debt and that must be accepted by the debtor as proper payment.

lender An individual or institution that makes a business in providing funds to others for a fee.

less than carload See *lcl*.

let To lease or hire out a building or equipment to another. To award a contract for goods or services. *Law* An obstruction or hindrance.

letter of credit *Commerce, Finance* An instrument

issued by a bank to guarantee the credit of a buyer up to a specified amount, usually to protect the buyer in international trade.

letter quality *Computers* Descriptive of a printer image that emulates the quality of a good typewriter.

leverage *Finance* The use of borrowed money to finance expansion and increase the profitability of a company. The relation of debt to equity in a company; the higher the long term debt, the greater the leverage.

leveraged buyout *Finance* The purchase of a corporation using borrowed funds that are largely secured by the assets of the firm being purchased.

levy The assessment and collection of taxes or other fees. The amount so assessed.

liability Any legal obligation, as money owed, or a judgment requiring the payment of compensation for damages. Anything that works to ones disadvantage. *Accounting* Any of the debts of an individual or business.

liability insurance Protective coverage for an individual or business against losses suffered by claims of injury to a third party including those arising from negligence, as for damage caused by a company's product or injury to a visitor in the company's plant. See also *casualty insurance*.

libel *Law* A tort wrong that consists of printing, or causing to be printed, any material that is slanderous, or that would in any way cause a person to be held in contempt or ridiculed. See also *slander*.

license Generally, a official granting of permission to do something, as to marry, conduct a business, practice a profession, etc. *Manufacturing* The granting of permission, usually for a royalty fee, to use a patented process and, in some cases, to advertise such use, as a clothing manufacturer who uses a well-known process to waterproof garments. Permission by a seller, for a buyer and user of brand name materials, to use the name to promote the buyer's product, as a photo processing company that promotes its use of a brand name print paper. *Marketing* An agreement that allows the use of copyrighted material for the promotion or decoration of a product, as a cartoon character on a child's lunch box.

lien *Law* A legal claim on property as the security for a debt.

LIFO; last in, first out *Accounting* A system for valuing inventory that presumes materials are removed in the reverse of the order that they are entered, thus matching the cost of the newest material with oldest revenue. In a time of rising prices it has been argued that this system properly reports a lower taxable income while minimizing the amount of money tied up in inventory. See also *FIFO*.

limited distribution *Marketing* Restricting the sale of a product to certain markets or to certain outlets within a market, often to control the way in which the product is sold, as by maintaining an image of exclusivity in order to maximize profit.

limited liability Generally, the restriction of possible losses from business reverses. In a partnership, the loss of a *limited partner* is restricted to the amount invested. Losses to the investors in a corporation are limited to the amount invested as well, unless an officer or shareholder has personally guaranteed an obligation of the corporation.

limited partnership A type of business firm in which certain partners have a financial interest, but play no active part in the operation of the organization; known as *limited partners*, their liability for company debts is limited to the capital they have invested. A limited partnership must have at least one general partner.

limiting Descriptive of that which restricts. *Computers* A device that, because of its slower speed or capacity, restricts the processing speed of the entire system. *Law* Of legislation that restricts or restrains, as of liability to the shareholders in a corporation or the powers of a municipality.

line Of those involved directly in company output. *Colloq.* Common term for the production line. *Marketing* The range of goods produced by a company, or stocked by a wholesaler or merchant.

line management Management personnel who oversee line functions, such as the production manager, plant manager, etc.

line of credit *Finance* An agreement by a financial institution to loan money as needed by a business up to a certain amount.

line personnel *Manufacturing* Those persons who work on a production line.

line printer *Computers* A high speed printer that prints a full line of copy at one time.

line supervisor *Manufacturing* One who directly supervises production employees, as a foreman, or floor walker.

link *Computers* The connection between two computers or a computer and peripherals. The connection between an embedded object and its source that permits updating in one instance to update all instances of the object.

linked documents *Computers* Records or files that are connected so that data from one will be automatically entered in another, such as billing records that are automatically added to the accounts receivable file.

liquid asset *Accounting, Finance* Cash or an asset that can be readily converted into cash.

liquidate *Finance* To dispose of, as a debt or other obligation by payment. To convert assets into cash. To settle the accounts of a business, as when it is being closed down.

liquidity *Finance* The ability of a business to meet its current obligations from cash on hand and assets that can be readily converted into cash.

list maintenance Of the process of adding, deleting and correcting entries to a mailing list. Considering that twenty percent of most lists change in the course of a year, list maintenance is critical to avoid wasting money and effort in mailing to non-existent addresses. In addition, a statistical analysis of the ratio of returns to pieces mailed may indicate that a particular list is targeting the wrong audience when, in fact, the figures are skewed by the number of dead listings.

list price *Marketing* The price quoted before discounts, sales, etc. The manufacturer's suggested retail price.

litigant *Law* A party involved in a lawsuit.

litigation *Law* Involvement in a lawsuit.

load *Computers* To call up a program or data to the computer's main memory from a storage device.

loan *Finance* A business transaction in which one party furnishes money or other assets to another in return for the promise of return or repayment plus an additional fee for profit.

lobbyist One who makes a business of influencing the members of a legislative or government administrative body as the representative of a special interest group.

local *Labor Relations* The local chapter of a labor union.

lockbox A post office box to which receivables are sent. The box number is listed on invoices as the address to which payment should be sent. The lockbox is used to separate receivables from the rest of the company's mail, to make processing more efficient, or to provide a centralized drop for a company that has facilities at more than one location. A company that sells its accounts receivables may prefer to conceal the fact by having payments sent to the factor in care of a lockbox in the company name. A financial institution that has loaned money against a company's receivables may also require a lockbox under their control; payments received are reported to the company and credited to its account.

locked in *Colloq.* Of that which is not likely to change under present circumstances, as a buyer who is dependent on a particular supplier because of that supplier's ability to deliver, or an agreement that has had all of the points of contention resolved.

lockout *Computers* Denial of access to the computer by a security system. In a program, temporary denial of access to commands during processing. *Labor Relations* Action by an employer to bar employees from working until an agreement has been reached, as for a labor contract.

logic Generally, correct or orderly reasoning. *Computers* The use of symbols in a formula to test the relationship between elements.

logic circuit *Computers* Computer circuitry that controls logic functions.

logic formula *Computers* A group of symbols that calculates to a logical *true* or *false*, as for a conditional branch.

logic operator *Computers* A symbol used in logic formulas.

log in or **log on** *Computers* To type in the password that allows access to the computer.

logo, logotype A distinguishing trademark or signature used by a company, often to identify its brands of merchandise.

long-range planning The process of setting budgets and goals for the achievement of future broad objectives, that is distinctive for its lack of detail. Long range planning involves setting objectives, and intermediate goals to reach those objectives, while maintaining a measure of flexibility in order to adjust for changes in business climate, technology, etc.

long-term contract Generally, any agreement, such as for labor, sales or the leasing of property that covers a period of more than one year.

long-term liability *Accounting, Finance* Any obligation, or portion of an obligation, that is not due for payment within twelve months. According to accepted accounting procedure, a debt that is to be paid in installments over a period of more than one year is reported as a long-term liability, except for the amount that is due in the current year.

lookup table *Computers* A set of variables arranged in a two dimensional array.

loop *Computers* A set of program instructions that are executed until a specific condition is met.

loop ender *Computers* A value expressed in a loop instruction to signal a branch and prevent unnecessary iterations of the loop.

loop feedback *Computers* The output value that modifies input for the next iteration of a loop instruction.

loophole *Law* A legal means of avoidance or escape, as from the provisions of a contract, or of an ordinance.

loosely coupled *Computers* Descriptive of computers that are connected, but that operate independently of one another.

loss leader *Marketing* Merchandise that is offered at a discount in order to attract customers in the hope that they will buy other goods as well.

low-ball *Marketing* To offer a price that is expected to be well below that of any other supplier, often to overcome all other considerations or resistance by a prospect who has a solid relationship with a competitor. While low-balling is a legitimate tactic to secure an order and the opportunity to prove that one is able to perform, companies often find themselves less willing to accept the loss once the order is placed and may seek to recoup their profits with overpriced extra charges.

lower of cost or market *Accounting* The conservative reporting of an asset value, that is, if the market value of an asset drops below its **book value**, the cost may be adjusted downward on financial reports to reflect the loss.

low grade Generally of inferior quality, as stocks, merchandise, etc.

lump sum distribution A single payment in full of an obligation that is normally expected to be doled out over time, as of an annuity or retirement fund.

luxury tax A tax on goods that are not considered a necessity.

machine dependent *Computers* A program or device that can only function on a particular computer or type of computer.

machine error *Computers* A program error caused by an equipment malfunction.

machine language *Computers* Instructions that can executed directly by a computer. Such instructions are extremely efficient and executed rapidly, but are very detailed, written in binary code and requiring a program statement for each machine action, so that programs are very difficult to write. Most programs are written in any one of a number of artificial languages that each have their own vocabulary and syntax, that somewhat emulate spoken English. The program so written must then be compiled, or translated, into machine language before being executed.

machine loading, machine loaded *Manufacturing* Of equipment that, once prepared for operation, automatically loads materials, parts, etc. for processing, such as an automatic camera in a design or print shop that loads a sheet of film for each shot by cutting it from a master roll. Of a type of production control or scheduling that takes into account the machines used in processing, the order in which they are used, and time required of each to process an order; delivery schedule is then determined by the availability of equipment when it is needed.

machine readable *Computers* Of a set of characters or symbols that can be read directly into a computer, usually by a scanner.

macro *Computers* A set of instructions that are executed by a single command or with a hot key combination.

magnetic disk *Computers* A computer storage medium. A hard disk or floppy disk.

mail fraud The use of the postal service to deliver material that is designed to deceive or to swindle the recipient, as by false claims for a product or an invoice for a product that was not ordered or sent.

mailing list A collection of names and addresses of individuals or organizations set up in such a manner that they can be used to address materials to be sent through the mail. A mailing list may be of customers, prospects, vendors, etc. and may be the property of the mailer or rented from an organization that trades in such lists. Rented lists vary greatly in value and cost of rental, based on their source, ranging from census tract lists that purport to include everyone living in a particular area, to those who fit a given **demographic** profile, to active buyers of mail order products. See also *list maintenance*.

mail merge *Computers* A program feature that combines a mailing list with the body of a letter.

mainframe *Computers* Of a large, fixed base computer that supports hundreds of users. The demand for such computers has fallen off as minicomputers and microcomputers grow more powerful and able to support multiple users and networks.

main memory *Computers* The internal memory of a computer from which programs are run.

maintenance The maintaining of buildings and equipment in good repair. See also *preventive maintenance*.

majority Of more than half, as a *majority* of the stockholders. *Law* Of the time when one reaches legal age.

majority shareholder A stockholder who owns more than half of the voting stock in a company and thus has a controlling interest. Often of a group that owns, or controls the votes of, more than half of the outstanding voting shares.

maker A person who signs or authorizes a transaction, as one who issues a check or signs a promissory note.

make-work Descriptive of a task that serves no purpose other than that of giving an otherwise idle person something to do.

malfeasance *Law* Committing that which is unlawful;

wrongdoing. See also *nonfeasance*.

malicious mischief The deliberate vandalism or destruction of the property of another.

malingerer One who feigns illness or injury to avoid work.

manage To control or direct, as an enterprise or a group of workers.

management agreement An employment contract. A contract between two companies engaged in a joint venture stipulating individual company responsibility and compensation for directing various phases or elements of the venture. A contract to direct certain aspects of a company's operations, usually joined with a company that specializes in such services, such as for accounting, human resources, training programs, etc.

management by exception The managerial concept that focuses attention on those events deviating from an acceptable pattern, such as a machine report that lists only those operations that produced below standard, or the posting of statements only to clients whose accounts are in arrears.

management by objective An administrative process whereby supervisors and workers jointly set goals and meet periodically to evaluate progress.

management consultant An individual or organization that specializes in the study and evaluation of the operation of other companies, for the purpose of offering advice to improve output, cut cost, reduce waste, etc.

Generally, management consultants specialize in a particular phase of operations, such as accounting and finance, materials handling, marketing and distribution, or labor relations, or in a particular industry, such as textiles, or printing.

management information system See *MIS*.

management prerogative Of those rights that the leadership of an organization holds to be theirs exclusively and not subject to collective bargaining, such as the scheduling of work or introduction of new processes.

mandate Generally, any commission or order to do something. *Law* A directive from a higher court to a lower one. Any contract that gives one the power to act for another.

mandatory Required; of that which is compulsory and not open to negotiation. *Labor Relations* Of the requirements for being hired, such as taking and passing a physical examination; for continued employment, such as obeying company rules or submitting to and passing a periodic test for the detection of controlled substances; and for being terminated, as by reaching retirement age. *Marketing* Of laws and regulations that govern the marketing of goods, such as requirements for special labeling on certain products.

man-hour A general term to express the output of one person in one hour on a particular job or operation. Professional services, such as those of an outside accountant or lawyer, are usually based on estimated or actual man-hours. *Manufacturing* An expression of output often used to determine the cost of a project or the number of persons required for completion on time.

manufacturer's software *Computers* A system program or driver that is supplied by the OEM for a specific piece of equipment.

manufacturing The process of constructing or fabricating a product, especially by machine and in large quantities.

manufacturing cost *Accounting* The cost to fabricate a product, including direct materials, direct labor and factory overhead.

margin *Accounting* Anticipated or actual profit; the difference between manufacturing cost and selling price.

marginal cost *Accounting* The cost of one additional unit of production, often expressed as **variable cost**.

marginal producer Of a product or company that is barely able to show a profit at the current price or volume level.

marginal revenue *Accounting* The increase in revenue from one additional unit of output. See also *marginal cost*.

marginal utility The satisfaction or utility gained from the consumption of one additional unit.

margin of profit Ratio of profit to sales, usually expressed as a percentage.

markdown A reduction in the selling price of goods. Sometimes, descriptive of a batch or assortment of goods that are odd sizes or out of style and are being sold off at a reduced price to clear inventory

market Generally, of any opportunity or potential opportunity to buy or sell; buyers and sellers meeting to trade. Any specific locale where goods are bought and sold.

marketability Of that which can be sold or is fit to be sold. *Finance* The ease with which an asset, such as stocks or real estate, can be converted to cash.

market analysis *Finance* Of any attempt to predict the future value of an investment, as a stock or bond, based on company performance or industry trends. *Marketing* Techniques for studying the characteristics and extent of the market for a product or group of products to predict future trends in order to formulate plans for expansion, diversification, etc.

market area *Marketing* The realm in which there is a demand or anticipated potential demand for a product, such as a geographic locale, a consumer group that fits a particular demographic profile, an industry, etc.

marketing All aspects of the advertising, merchandising and selling of goods and services.

marketing concept The strategy for promoting and selling a specific product or group of products, such as by identification with a particular lifestyle, by emphasis on benefits to users of the product, etc.

marketing director One who oversees all aspects of the marketing of a company's products, and to whom all personnel or departments responsible for marketing functions report.

market penetration *Marketing* The extent to which a particular product dominates or fails to dominate a market or market segment. A strategy intended to secure a larger share of a market or market segment by such means as aggressive advertising, promotion, etc.

marketplace Generally, anywhere that goods are

traded, although it may refer to a specific location or segment of a market. Often referring figuratively to the world of trade.

market potential *Marketing* The total value of goods or services that may be sold in a particular market or in all markets. For an individual supplier, *market potential* may be regarded as unrealized sales, that is, sales by the competition in the market area. *Market potential* may also refer to a market that has not been exploited, as by a new use for a product.

market price Generally, the current prevailing price at which a product is being traded, or the price determined by supply and demand as contrasted to a price set by company policy.

market profile The configuration of data that describes the prospective individual or organizational buyer or user of a product, as by lifestyle, type of business, etc.

market research Investigation into the characteristics of a potential market, such as location, size, etc., and those in the market, such as age, education, income level, etc.

market segmentation Dividing the market for a product into separate categories according to such factors as geographic location, individual or company buyer, end use, age of user, etc. Such segmentation allows for efficient and effective advertising, promotion, customer service, etc.

market share *Marketing* The portion of the total market, or market segment, controlled by a particular company, usually expressed as a percentage of the total market.

market value *Finance* The price that goods in inventory or equipment would bring if offered for sale at a given time.

markup *Marketing* An amount added to the cost of goods to cover overhead and profit, usually expressed as a percentage of cost.

mass media Of communication systems that reach a very large audience, as radio, television, certain publications, etc.

mass production *Manufacturing* Of the fabrication of large quantities of goods on automated equipment.

matching *Accounting* The concept of financial reporting that strives for the pairing of revenue with the expenses associated with the generation of that revenue.

material Generally, a thing of significance or physical presence. The substances that, with labor and overhead, go into the cost of a project or the manufacture of a product. *Law* That of sufficient importance that it may influence a judgment.

material budget *Manufacturing* A list of those supplies, or the cost of supplies, that have been allocated for a project or the fabrication of a batch of goods.

material cost *Accounting* The actual cost of supplies used for a particular project or in the fabrication of a batch of goods. Depending on company policy, the cost may be the amount invoiced by the vendor, or it may include some overhead for storage and handling, often applied as a percentage of the invoiced value.

materials handling Any manipulation and recording

of the disposition of supplies in the plant, including the receiving, storing, and movement of raw goods; the moving, packing, shipping, and storage of finished goods; and disposal of waste.

nath coprocessor *Computers* A chip that works in conjunction with the CPU to perform high speed arithmetic calculations.

nathematical operator A symbol that governs an arithmetic computation.

natrix *Computers* A pattern for comparison of elements in optical character recognition. A two dimensional array.

naturity *Finance* Of the due date of an obligation.

naxim A brief expression of a general rule, truth, or principle.

nechanic's lien *Law* A security on property granted to one who has furnished labor or materials for the improvement of the property.

nechanization *Manufacturing* The performance of tasks by machine. Of the conversion of operations from handwork to machine.

nedia Plural of medium. All of the means of communicating with the general public, as radio, television, publications, etc. *Marketing* All of the means of communication that carry advertising in addition to entertainment, news, etc.

nedia blitz *Marketing* Saturation advertisement of a product in a market or markets that comprises numerous ads in all media designed to reach as many people as possible in the market area.

media event *Marketing* A public appearance or happening that has been staged to garner publicity through the news media.

mediation *Labor Relations* Intervention in a dispute between labor and management by a third party, often a government official. The findings of a *mediator* are not binding.

mediator *Labor Relations* A person who attempts to assist parties to a dispute in reaching a settlement, often one who specializes in such service.

medium Singular of *media*.

megabyte, MB *Computers* One million bytes.

megahertz, MHz *Computers* One million cycles per second.

memo, memorandum A short note written by one as a reminder or something or as a record of events. An informal communication, usually between parties within a company. *Accounting* A preliminary document, as a *memo billing* sent with a shipment of goods. A notice or directive that authorizes some action, as the return of damaged or disputed goods. *Law* A brief, preliminary statement of the terms of an agreement or contract.

memory *Computers* A device in which data can be stored and accessed at a later time. *ROM* or *read-only memory* refers to an area of storage where the data is permanently imprinted, that is, it can be read, but not altered, as that which is built into the computer to control its basic functions. *RAM* or *random access memory* is dynamic volatile memory that must be constantly refreshed to be retained, as the area in a computer where programs are loaded for execution; *random access* refers to very fast memory of which any part can be addressed independent of the previous access. *Permanent memory* or *permanent storage* refers to memory in the computer, or on a removable device such as a disk, where data is stored; data may be changed by the operator and the memory is not dynamic, so that it is not lost when the power is off.

memory card *Computers* A computer add-on that provides additional storage.

memory resident *Computers* Descriptive of a program or utility that is loaded in RAM. See also *TSR*.

menu *Computers* Generally, a reference to a list of options from which the user can select

menu driven *Computers* Descriptive of a program that is easy to learn and use because it affords the user the option of selecting program options from a list, in contrast to those programs that require the user to learn numerous commands.

menial One who is a servant or servile, or a person who is employed in a lowly position. Of the tasks performed by such a person.

merchandise Things bought and sold. The act of buying and selling. *Marketing* To advertise or promote the sale of goods.

merchandise allowance Payment, or credit on account, for goods that have been returned.

merchandising *Marketing* Promoting the sale of goods through advertising and publicity, proper display and support at the point of sale, programs for discounting to buyers or consumers, etc.

merchandising allowance *Marketing* A standard offer by a manufacturer or distributor to share a portion of the cost of local advertising or promotion with the retailer.

merchant One engaged in the business of buying and selling goods at a profit, especially a shopkeeper who sells at retail.

merge Generally, to absorb, or join together, often with a loss of identity of the elements as they existed before the merge, as of two companies. See also *merger*. *Computers* To combine, as a file or database. See also *mail merge*.

merged sort *Computers* To combine and arrange in a particular order, as alphabetically, sets of database files.

merger A blending of two or more companies by acquisition, in which one company purchases others and they are absorbed into the parent company, or by consolidation, in which a new corporation is formed to absorb the merging companies.

merit pay, merit raise *Labor Relations* An addition to a standard wage that is awarded for outstanding performance on the job.

metered mail Mail that is stamped by a postage meter.

methods study Examination, usually by a third party, of the established systems, formal and informal, for accomplishing tasks throughout a company. The purpose of such a study is to find and eliminate the pockets of waste caused by miscommunication, misdirection, etc. through formalizing procedures that require more uniform action or results, and eliminating any structures or rules that are outdated or tend to make a task more complicated or difficult than it needs to be.

metric system A decimal system of weights and measures in which the basic unit of weight is the gram, of measure is the meter, and of capacity is the liter.

metropolitan area The broad region that includes a city and the surrounding area that is economically linked to it.

microcomputer A computer that is operated by a single integrated circuit called a microprocessor. Various types of the microcomputer are the desktop computer, laptop computer and notebook computer.

microprocessor An integrated circuit that holds the complete central processing unit for a microcomputer.

MIDI, musical instrument digital interface *Computers* The protocol for interaction between a digitized musical instrument and a computer.

middleman *Commerce, Marketing* One who purchases goods from a manufacturer to sell to a retailer or direct to the consumer.

middle management Generally a reference to those who hold administrative positions somewhere between top management and line supervisors.

migratory worker One who moves from place to place to find work, as an agricultural worker who follows the harvest.

milk *Colloq.* To exploit a situation for gain, such as by eating in the finest restaurants to take advantage of an expense account.

mill *Accounting, Finance* One tenth of a cent; from the Latin for thousandth, or one thousandth of a dollar.

mineral rights An agreement that conveys privilege to

remove oil or other resources from the land and sell them for profit. Ownership of mineral rights may be held or conveyed separately from ownership of the land itself.

minicomputer *Computer* A small computer that is between a mainframe and a microcomputer in size, and that is designed to support multiple users. Mainframes, in many instances, are being replaced by powerful new minicomputers, which in turn are increasingly being replaced by networked microcomputers.

minimum wage *Labor Relations* The lowest hourly rate that can be paid to a worker who is covered by a contract, in a particular job classification. *Law* The lowest hourly rate that can be paid to a worker according to the provisions of federal or state law, usually in reference to the federal Fair Labor Standards Act that sets a minimum rate for those workers covered.

minor *Law* Of one who has not reached **majority** as specified by the law of the state governing. One who is a minor faces certain restrictions of action, such as for entering into marriage or joining the armed forces without consent.

minority interest Of the portion of a company owned by those who, in the aggregate, hold less than half of a company's voting stock.

minutes The record of transactions at a meeting, especially those of a corporation, scheduled to conduct official business, as a shareholder's meeting or a meeting of the board of directors.

MIS, Management Information System *Computers* A

system designed to provide timely and accurate reports for management to use as an aid in decision-making. Such a system requires correlation and integration of information gathering, data entry, and data processing.

misdemeanor *Law* Any minor transgression, such as failure to comply with a local ordinance, that carries a relatively light penalty.

mismanagement The failure to properly fulfill administrative duties either through neglect or malice. Mismanagement may refer simply to poor performance in directing a single, small project or it may be far more serious, as in the misappropriation of company funds.

misrepresentation Generally, false or misleading information. *Marketing* A statement or implication in product advertising, whether by accident or malice, that may cause injury to a buyer and become the basis for litigation, as by claiming a product is safe when, in fact, it contains chemicals that can cause illness.

mistake Generally, an error. *Law* An act or failure to act that may be grounds for revocation of a contract, or dismissal of a charge of liability against another.

mitigation A moderation or making less severe. *Law* A petition to a court for a reduction of damages on the basis of evidence that the injured party is not entitled to the full amount of the damages.

mix Generally, a blending of diverse elements. In business, often a reference to the proportion of each element in a total. *Finance* A factor in predicting a company's future strength and prospects, as by judging what the product mix will be based on anticipated demand and predicting profitability based on that mix, for example, a company's prospects may be declining despite anticipated sales increases if demand for its most profitable line is falling as the demand for less profitable items increases. *Manufacturing* Of the relative quantity of each of the company's products that is to be produced in a given period, especially as it influences the allocation of resources in order to manufacture them efficiently. *Marketing* Of the share of each of the company's products sold in each market, an important factor in planning promotion. Of the relative amount of advertising placed with each medium for a particular campaign, especially as it relates to heavy reliance on one.

mixed media See *multimedia*.

mixed signals *Colloq.* Unclear indicators of what is correct, especially those based on contradictory messages or reports. For example, reports of increasing demand for a product in a market where the number of persons fitting the demographic profile of a user is declining.

mnemonics Techniques for aiding memory. *Computers* Commands designated so as to make remembering their function easier, as *Q* for *quit*, or *P* for *print*.

modeling The process of formulating a mathematical representation that can be manipulated to show the consequence of change. For example, one might use a model of the income statement for the previous year to illustrate what the results would have been if the product mix were changed, if a product had been dropped, etc. as an aid to planning. Budgets for future periods can then be manipulated to test the effect of changes in `product mix, addition of new equipment, changes in the cost of materials, etc.

modem *Computers* Modulator/demodulator; a device that converts electronic signals, especially the conversion of discrete data from a computer to analog data for transmission by telephone lines that is converted back to discrete data by the receiver.

momentum Generally, the driving force of a thing in motion. Descriptive of a condition in which the strength of movement is seen as an influence on the tendency to continue moving in the same direction, as by a strengthening economy.

monetary *Finance* Of that which concerns money.

money *Finance* In general, any medium of exchange that has recognized value, as coined or printed currency, bank notes, checks, precious metals, property, etc.

monitor Generally, anything or anyone that observes, regulates, or supervises. *Computers* A video screen that allows the user to view processing and interact with the computer. A program that oversees and manages the operation of other programs.

monopoly Sole control of a particular line of goods or services in a given market or the means to control distribution and price

moonlighting Having a second job, full- or part-time, in addition to a regular job.

morale A spirit of confidence; the mental state of a person or group in relation to a positive mental attitude.

moral obligation Of a commitment that will be honored because it is the right thing to do and represents the way in which reasonable people deal with one another rather than because of a legal requirement.

mortgage *Finance* The pledge of real estate as collateral for the payment of a loan.

mortgage insurance Any protection for the lender, or mortgagee, against loss, such as restitution for damages to the property, for damages resulting from foreclosure, or from the death of the mortgagor.

motion study An examination of the flow of work, material, etc. on an assembly line or throughout a manufacturing plant in order to make production more cost effective.

motivation The inner drive that causes one to act in a certain manner.

motivational research *Labor Relations* The study and analysis of those things that influence, or are of the greatest importance, to workers so that they might be used to encourage better performance on the job. *Marketing* Studies that attempt to determine what might influence a consumer to buy a particular product.

motor freight Trucks or trucking lines in contrast to the railroad.

mouse *Computers* A device for extremely rapid and random movement of the cursor on a monitor screen. In addition, some mouses can be programmed, so that a mouse button in combination with other keys can execute a series of keystrokes.

multimedia *Computers* Of the combining of sound and video images in a computer program or presentation. *Marketing* Of an advertising or promotional campaign that utilizes more than one medium, as television, radio and direct mail, often with messages that reinforce one another.

multinational corporation Of a corporation that operates production plants or branches in more than one country.

multiplexer *Computers* A system that manages signals between two or more devices simultaneously.

multitasking *Computers* The ability of a CPU to execute two or more programs or routines at the same time, either by independent processing or by interleaving.

multi-user system *Computers* A system designed to mange input and output from several terminals at the same time.

Murphy's law The maxim that if there is anything that can go wrong, it will, named for the engineer who originally expressed the sentiment in 1949.

national bank *Finance* A bank chartered by the federal government through the Comptroller of the Currency.

national brand *Marketing* A product that is widely distributed, in contrast to a local or regional brand.

Natural Bureau of Standards A government agency established in 1901 that conducts the research that is the basis for a national system of weights and measures, and performs other services for science and industry in the realm of testing and evaluation.

nationalization The confiscation of private assets by

a government.

Nation Labor Relations Act *Labor Relations* Federal regulation that officially recognized collective bargaining by providing for the supervision of representative elections and outlawed unfair labor practices by employers.

Nation Labor Relations Board *Labor Relations* Agency created by the National Labor Relations Act that monitors the dealings between employers and the representatives of employees.

natural monopoly Generally, an enterprise that dominates a market because of conditions that limit the entry of other producers. One who raises a crop that will only grow in a limited part of the country, or who manufactures a product that is protected by patent, enjoys a natural monopoly. Such a monopoly may be legislated when it is in the public good, as by granting the right for a public utility to operate in a particular area.

natural resources Those materials that are gleaned from nature.

near letter quality, NLQ *Computers* A designation of the ability of a printer to emulate the quality of reproduction one would expect from a typewriter.

negative cash flow *Accounting* A condition characterized by a period during which a business paid out more cash than it received. A negative cash flow for a single period does not necessarily indicate a problem, as it may simply reflect a higher than normal level of credit sales in relation to expenditures and the company may have adequate cash or credit line to cover the shortfall. In addition, a period of rapid expansion may require buying from new vendors with whom credit has not been established, so that the proportion of expenditures to receipts is out of line. Over the longer term, however, a negative cash flow may indicate a failure to react quickly to increases in cost, improper management of accounts receivable, etc.

negligence *Law* The failure to exercise due care that results in injury or damages to another.

negotiable instrument A written agreement that contains a promise to pay a specific sum on demand or at a fixed time in the future and that can be transferred easily from one party to another.

negotiated price Any charge for goods or services that is arrived at by agreement between buyer and seller, often occasioned by special needs of the buyer, as for extended credit, special packaging or a custom product, or by conditions, such as the sellers desire to break into a market or a need for additional volume.

negotiation Generally, a bargaining or conferring. *Commerce* Bargaining between buyer and seller to arrive at a mutually agreeable price and terms. *Finance* The transfer of a **negotiable instrument** from one party to another. *Labor Relations* Bargaining in an attempt to reach agreement on the terms of a labor contract. *Marketing* Bargaining with media representatives to derive the best exposure for a favorable price.

nepotism *Labor Relations* Preferential treatment to relatives, especially in their appointment to lucrative positions in a company or department. Many

net

companies bar or place restrictions on the hiring of those who are related in order to avoid the problems that such hiring can create.

net Of that which remains after deductions, as *sales* less *returns and allowances, profit* after deduction of *taxes, shipping weight* after deduction for *wrapping* or *container*, etc. The strict definition of similar items, as *net sales* or *net profit*, often vary from one company to another, and sometimes from one report to another, depending on how the term is being used, company policy, etc.

net assets *Accounting, Finance* The value of all of a company's assets, less liabilities. Also known as *owner's equity* or *net worth.*

net asset value *Finance* Generally, the book value of a share of stock, especially as applied to a mutual fund, calculated by deducting the value of intangible assets from net assets and dividing by the number of outstanding shares.

net cost The original cost of an asset less anything realized from its disposition, usually of an asset that is being sold or traded in, as the first step to determining profit or loss on the transaction for tax purposes.

net income *Accounting, Finance* Generally, revenue less all expenses; net profit or loss. Often a provisional amount, that is, qualified on a financial report as *before sales expense, before administrative cost, before taxes, etc.*

net loss *Accounting, Finance* A loss recorded on the income statement after allowance for taxes, extraordinary charges, etc.

net profit *Accounting, Finance* Profit after allowance for taxes, extraordinary charges, etc.

net quick assets *Finance* The amount by which *quick assets*, that is, cash, accounts receivable and marketable securities, exceed current liabilities. In effect, it is a measure of a company's ability to meet its current obligations with easily convertible assets if sales were to dry up.

net realizable value *Accounting* The amount that might be obtained from the sale of an asset after deducting any expenses associated with the sale, such as the cost of making the asset salable.

net sales *Accounting, Financing* Revenue less any returns and allowances.

network Generally, any group of persons or things that are connected with each other for some purpose. In business, often used to express an informal system of contacts that may be of help from time to time. *Computers* A number of computers, terminals, printers, scanners, plotters, or other peripherals that are connected in such a way that they can communicate with each other.

network server *Computers* A computer that stores and manages programs and data for other computers in the network.

net worth *Accounting, Finance* The value of all of an individual or a company's assets, less their liabilities. Also known as *owner's equity*.

new issue *Finance* Of stocks or bonds being sold by a corporation for the first time. *New issue* may refer to an initial offering by a private company that is going public, or an addition issue to secure operating capital or funds for expansion, by a public company.

niche Generally, a place that is especially suited to the thing in it. *Marketing* Of a particular market or specialty area where a company finds it profitable to concentrate its efforts. Niche marketing offers a concentration of clients in an atmosphere of limited competition.

no-fault insurance Of a type of protection, mandated by law in certain states, wherein losses to all parties, as in an automobile accident, are covered with no regard to who is at fault.

noise *Computers* A reference to extraneous and undesirable signals that interfere with transmission.

nolo contendere *Law* A plea allowed a defendant in a criminal case, in which the charges are not contested, but without admission of guilt.

nominal Generally, descriptive of that which is in name only; sometimes, an expression of that which is so slight as to be, virtually, in name only.

nominal damages *Law* A small award in recognition that a wrong was done when there is no proof of significant recoverable damages.

nominal wage A wage stated as an amount paid, without consideration of purchasing power.

nonconforming use *Law* Utilization of a parcel of land in a manner that is not in keeping with the local zoning ordinance, such as for a commercial enterprise that is located in a residential area, that occurs when the use existed before the restrictive ordinance was passed.

noncontributory *Insurance* Of a company medical, life, or retirement plan that is funded completely by the employer.

noncontrollable cost *Accounting* Of expenses that are not influenced or may be influenced only marginally by a particular individual or set of circumstances. Such costs are removed from consideration, for example, when evaluating the performance of a supervisor who cannot be held accountable for the cost of rent or utilities.

nondestructive read *Computers* Access of a data file while maintaining a copy of the file in storage.

nonfeasance *Law* Failure to do that which duty requires. See also *malfeasance*.

nonperformance *Law* Failure to perform according to agreement, as a contract.

non printing character *Computers* A command or formatting character in a computer document.

nonproductive Generally, of that which does not contribute to output, often of that which is wasteful of resources. *Accounting* Descriptive of those functions that cannot be directly identified with the fabrication of goods or the providing of service; overhead.

nonprofit Of an organization that is not formed for the express purpose of making a profit for its investors. Such an organization is often formed for some humanitarian, scientific or educational purpose, as a hospital or foundation, and is usually exempt from taxes.

nonrecurring *Accounting, Finance* Of a line item on a financial report that is unique and not expected to occur again, such as for income from the sale of equipment, or a one-time charge associated with the cost of a lawsuit.

nonvoting stock *Finance* Of preferred or other special issue stock that does not qualify the shareholder to have vote in corporate elections.

norm Normal; within the realm of standard practice, behavior, achievement, etc.

normal price *Commerce* The price at which a particular product or service is traded when there is no fluctuation attributable to excess supply or demand.

normal profit *Finance* The profit level at which a producer will continue in business without significant change. A higher profit level attracts competition that will have the effect of lowering profit; a lower profit level may make other investments more attractive to the producer.

normal spoilage *Manufacturing* Wasted material or rejected product that is expected and unavoidable in a fabricating or manufacturing operation under usual conditions.

normal wear and tear *Accounting* Of that which is intended to be covered by depreciation allotted for the gradual decrease in value of equipment; there is no provision for unexpected damage to the equipment.

no-strike clause *Labor Relations* A provision in a labor contract stipulating that the workers will not strike as long as the employer lives up to the terms of the contract.

notary, notary public A public official who is authorized to authenticate documents, take depositions, perform marriages, etc.

notation *Computers* The system of words, symbols, mnemonics, etc. used to write computer programs.

note *Finance* A written promise acknowledging a debt and specifying the terms for repayment.

notebook computer *Computers* A portable computer with a monitor screen and keyboard contained in a single unit; the smallest of the general purpose computers. See also **microcomputer**.

notes payable *Accounting, Finance* Obligations in the form of debts due to others as shown on the balance sheet.

notes receivable *Accounting, Finance* An asset on the balance sheet in the form of debts due from others.

not for profit See **nonprofit**.

notice to quit *Law* Notification to a tenant that rental property is to be vacated.

nuisance *Law* A condition that poses or may pose a danger to others, or that interferes with the free use of one's property.

null and void *Law* That cannot be legally enforced; invalid, as the terms of a contract that are contrary to law.

number cruncher One capable of carrying out a project that involves a large number of complex calculations, generally descriptive of an accountant, often with the aid of a computer.

objective Without bias or personal prejudice. Intent or purpose, as of a marketing plan.

object linking and embedding, OLE *Computers* Connecting text or graphics data between documents and applications—linking implies that a change of data in one position changes all occurrences of the same data.

obligation *Law* A duty, as to pay a debt according to

an agreement. The contract or other document that outlines the terms of such an agreement.

obsolescence The condition of being outdated or useless because of advancing technology.

occupation One's trade or profession.

occupational disease A affliction that is associated with those who engage in a particular type of work.

occupational hazard Conditions associated with certain jobs that expose the workers to the danger of injury on the job.

OCR, optical character recognition *Computers* Any of the systems or techniques for reading characters or symbols from hard copy and translating them into digital data for manipulation, such as a system that accepts input from a retail store checkout scan of product labels to ring up the sale, adjust inventory, etc. A program capability that involves reading graphic text from a hard copy or computer file, and translating it into characters that can be manipulated by the user.

octal A numbering system in base eight.

OEM, original equipment manufacturer *Commerce, Computers* The manufacturer, as contrasted to the distributor, of a particular product.

off-brand *Marketing* A product that emulates a popular brand, often of inferior quality and less expensive.

offer An expression of interest as the first step toward entering into an agreement. That which is presented for consideration. To present for sale, or bid on that which is for sale.

office automation *Computers* Use of the computer to

assist in the tasks associated with running a business, such as bookkeeping, inventory control, maintaining mailing lists, etc.

office management The organization and administration of a company's offices.

off-line *Computers* Of peripheral equipment that is not turned on or that is not directly connected to or controlled by the computer. Of data that is not entered directly into the computer, but rather to a storage device, such as a tape, which is then processed by the computer.

offset *Accounting* That which sets off or balances as the offsetting credit and debit entries to the ledger. *Finance, Law* The right of a bank to confiscate deposited funds to cover a loan that is in default, called the *right of offset*.

offshore *Financial* Of any financial organization that has its headquarters outside the U.S. Of subsidiaries of U.S. firms that operate outside the U.S. to avoid heavy regulation.

off the books *Colloq.* Transactions, such as barters or payments for labor, that are not recorded in order to avoid taxes.

old boy network *Colloq.* Of the relationship that exists between certain groups of men who favor each other in business transactions and shut others out.

oligopoly A market that is dominated by a few large suppliers, as for automobiles.

ombudsman A public official or representative of a private organization who investigate the complaints of private citizens.

on account *Accounting, Finance* A payment made to

partly liquidate a debt. A sale on credit, or charged to the client's account.

on consignment *Marketing* Of goods that are delivered to a merchant for sale; unsold goods are returned to the manufacturer or wholesaler.

on demand *Finance* Of a note or other obligation without a fixed payment date and for which payment may be requested at the pleasure of the holder of the obligation.

one-time buyer *Marketing* A purchaser of advertising who is contracting for a limited number of spots or insertions and is therefore not eligible for volume discounts.

on-line *Computers* Of data entry or peripherals that are connected directly to the main computer. Of equipment that is turned on.

on order Goods that have been requisitioned, but not yet received.

on-pack *Marketing* Of a premium that is attached to the outside of the package containing a product. Many marketers have reservations about the effectiveness of the on-pack because of the tendency of the premium to disappear before the product is sold. See also *in-pack*.

on-sale date *Marketing* The day on which a dated publication is to go on sale, and any remaining copies of the previous issues are to be returned to the distributor. The day on which a new product is placed on sale, often coordinated with an advertising and promotion campaign.

on speculation *Marketing* Preliminary studies, artwork, presentations, etc. prepared by an advertising agency at no charge in the hopes of securing business.

on-the-job training Learning a trade while working at it, often part of a formal training program.

op code, operation code *Computers* A symbol or set of characters that directs the computer to execute a command.

open *Computers* Of a file that has been copied from memory storage to RAM and is available to the user for updating or editing.

open account *Accounting* Descriptive of a client's account that contains unpaid charges. *Marketing* Sales terms that allow the client to buy on credit.

open bidding Tendering a price for goods, services, a project, etc. that is open to negotiation. See also *sealed bid.*

open-end contract *Commerce* A contract to furnish goods or services of an indefinite quantity for an unspecified period, providing for termination after proper notice by either party. *Labor Relations* A labor contract that has no fixed termination date, but a provision that calls for renegotiation at the request of either party after proper notification.

open house In real estate, a means of showing property that is kept open to prospective buyers for inspection on specified dates. *Marketing* A means of promoting a company or its goods, especially the introduction of a new product, by creating a media event around a tour of the company facilities for prospective clients and a group of dignitaries or celebrities.

open order *Commerce* An order that has not been

filled or canceled.

open shop *Labor Relations* An organization where workers are free to choose to become members of the union or not. In an open shop, non-union workers are employed under the same conditions as union workers and, though they lack the advocacy of the union when filing a grievance, share most of the same benefits as union members. See also *closed shop, right to work, union shop*.

open stock *Commerce* Descriptive of merchandise that is kept in stock by a merchant, wholesaler, or manufacturer. Often of merchandise that can be purchased singly or as part of a set, such as china, cutlery, or crystal.

operating budget Estimated expenditures for transacting company business at the level of production forecast by the sales projection for a given period.

operating cycle A characteristic model of business activity in which cash or other assets are converted into inventory and ultimately into a product or service that is, in turn, sold for cash or other assets. The length of time from the purchase of raw materials for production until they are sold as finished goods.

operating expense *Accounting* The costs incurred in the normal conduct of a business, as distinguished from capital investment, the cost to acquire the means of production, or any extraordinary expenses.

operating income *Accounting* Revenues generated in the course of supplying the goods and services that are the stock in trade of a business.

operating loss *Accounting* Losses sustained in the normal conduct of business, that do not include any unusual losses, as from the sale of equipment, from a court order to pay damages, etc.

operating profit *Accounting* Profits resulting from the normal conduct of business, that do not proceed from any extraordinary transactions, as the sale of an asset, a windfall judgment, etc.

operating system Generally, the procedures and practices that determine the manner in which an organization conducts its affairs. *Computers* The program that provides a platform for the control of the functions of the computer, such as DOS, OS/2, etc.

operation Generally, any procedure or activity that is one of a series of similar activities serving to reach an objective, as *the painting operation* in an automobile assembly plant. The series of actions taken as a whole, as *a manufacturing operation.* Sometimes, referring to the site where such activities take place.

opinion Generally, an expression of that which is not certain, but which seems probable or likely valid. In business, it is often the valuation or judgment of an expert hired for examination of a particular matter, as the statement of an auditor after reviewing the company financial records. *Law* A formal statement by the court regarding the law that has bearing on a case.

opinion leader *Marketing* Descriptive of one who influences a number of others in the selection of goods and whose endorsement of a product is, therefore, highly valued.

opportunity cost Generally, a means to compare the differences in return one might expect from the selection among alternative investments; the amount that is forfeit by selecting one alternative over another. *Accounting* Potential income that is lost by resources committed to accounts receivable, inventory, etc. *Finance* In the evaluation of investment, as for new equipment or buildings, the amount that is forfeit by not committing resources to the best alternative investment.

opt Generally, to choose or select, as to opt for an alternative. To *opt out* is to decline, or back out, as of a commitment, membership, etc.

optical character recognition *Computers* Any of the systems or techniques for reading characters or symbols from hard copy and translating them into digital data for manipulation, such as a system that accepts input from a retail store checkout scan of product labels to ring up the sale, adjust inventory, etc. A program capability that involves reading graphic text from a hard copy or computer file, and translating it into characters that can be manipulated by the user.

optimal Descriptive of a course of action or solution to a problem that presents the best return for the least risk.

optimization Generally, to make the best use of, to get the most out of, or to accumulate as much as possible of something. Making the best use of facilities so as to maximize profit or output.

optimum capacity The volume of production in a manufacturing operation that results in the lowest unit cost. See also *ideal capacity*.

option The right to choose or the act of choosing. Any of a number of alternatives or alternative courses of action available to one who must make a decision. *Computers* Any of the features of a program or application available to the user. *Finance* The right, acquired for consideration, to buy or sell an asset at an agreed price within a specified period. If the option is not executed within the specified time, it expires and the owner of the option forfeits the cost of the option. *Insurance* Any of the choices that may be made for exemptions or additional coverage that are not an integral part of the basic coverage of an insurance policy. *Marketing* Any feature that is not a standard part of a product or service, but that may be included for an extra charge.

oral contract An agreement that is not documented in writing. In most cases, oral contracts are valid, but are difficult to enforce because of the difficulty in establishing precise wording and intent.

order Generally, of a logical sequence or the act of arranging in logical sequence. *Commerce* Authorization to fabricate or provide a product or service for an agreed price. The goods or services so provided. *Computers* A program or application feature that arranges data in a sequence according to the user's instructions. *Law* A charge or command from a court or jurisdiction.

order entry *Commerce* The process of recording an order and performing the necessary tasks to assure that the order is filled. The procedure for order entry varies greatly from one company to another and from one industry to another. For example, an order for merchandise from a catalog house may require only an entry to the client's account, a warehouse order that authorizes picking, packing, and shipping of the merchandise, and a subsequent confirmation of shipping charges to post to the client's account. On the other hand, an order for custom fabricated goods may require the preparation of work orders for the plant, purchase orders and requisitions for materials, confirmation of delivery dates, etc.

order form *Commerce* A pre-printed form used to submit a request for merchandise from a wholesaler or manufacturer. *Marketing* In direct mail marketing, the form filled out by a client to request merchandise. Such forms are designed to simplify the process for the client, often requiring only that options be checked off and designed so that the order form itself becomes the mailer that conveys the order to the seller.

order number *Commerce* An identification number used to track a request for merchandise and the charges associated with it.

ordinance *Law* A statute or regulation enacted by government body, especially of a municipality.

ordinary and necessary Descriptive of an expense that qualifies as deductible for income tax purposes, and that implies the expenditure was not frivolous or for personal gain.

ordinary course of business A conditional qualifier descriptive of any activity that is necessary and incidental to the conduct of business, and that by implication excludes any activity that does not so qualify.

ordinary life *Insurance* An insurance policy that provides a death benefit as well as a cash surrender value that builds throughout the life of the policy and is paid out at a specified age or after a number of years in force.

organization An association of individuals joined together for a specific purpose, as a business, social club, charity, etc.

organizational structure The manner is which the offices and lines of authority or a company or other establishment are arranged.

organization chart A graphic representation of the positions, departments, etc. in an organization and the lines of authority and communication between them.

organization cost, organization expense *Accounting* The costs to start a business or form a legal corporation, such as for legal fees, registration fees, franchise costs, etc. An intangible asset account that is carried on the company's books and may be amortized.

organized labor *Labor Relations* Collectively, the labor unions that engage in collective bargaining for their members.

orientation program Any program for introduction or familiarization with a company, environment, etc. Often referring to a briefing of new employees, orientation may be as simple as a tour of the office or plant, or it may be a series of meetings to familiarize an employee with every facet of the company's operation and his or her part in it.

original cost *Accounting* The purchase price of an asset plus all of the costs associated with bringing it on line, including shipping costs, modifications, testing, etc.

original entry *Accounting* The first recording of a financial transaction in a journal which may also contain an explanation or authorization for the entry.

original equipment Tools, supplies, parts, etc. that are sold to a fabricator to be joined to, and sold as part of, the final product, as the tires on a car or a monitor sold with a computer.

original equipment manufacturer Designating of one who makes a product that is furnished to another for resale to the consumer as an independent device or as part of another product.

OS/2, Operating System 2 *Computers* A program that controls all of the basic operations of the computer.

other expense *Accounting* An income statement account that reports extraordinary cost, that is, charges not associated with the normal conduct of business, or that would normally be matched against revenues of another period.

other income *Accounting* An income statement account that reports extraordinary revenue, that is, income not associated with the normal conduct of business, such as for a manufacturer receiving income for the sale of equipment or the rental of property.

outlet A location for distribution to the consumer, as a store or market. Sometimes, a shop that sells the goods, often seconds, of a particular manufacturer. Originally such outlet stores were located near a manufacturer or on the manufacturer's premises;

however, increased popularity has prompted their establishment throughout the country, often in malls dedicated to such outlet stores.

out-of-pocket cost Generally, descriptive of expenses that have not been budgeted, or those for minor, miscellaneous items. *Accounting* Indicating of the direct costs of manufacturing, often used as the basis for the decision to accept a contract at a marginal price level. *Marketing* A miscellaneous allowance in a promotional budget to cover incidental expenses.

out of stock Descriptive of merchandise that is not immediately available when sought by a buyer. *Out of stock* implies a temporary condition that will be corrected by a reorder, a shipment in transit, or re-stocking by the manufacturer, rather than that the item is no longer available.

output The quantity of production achieved by a fabricator. *Computers* The results of processed data. Output may take such forms as personalized letters produced by combining copy for a standard letter with information contained in a database, financial or other reports for management, the checks and backup reports that make up a payroll, a production schedule, etc.

output device *Computers* A peripheral unit that delivers information to the user, such as a printer or plotter.

outside director Any member of the board of directors who is not employed by the company, often a lawyer, other professional, or business leader whose diverse opinions and contacts are of value to the firm.

outsourcing Buying the products or services of another firm, usually for a component of the buyer's product. Frequently used to designate only the purchase of goods or services to supplement in-house production when a company facility is overbooked.

outstanding *Finance* Designating of a debt that has not been paid or collected, or an instrument that has not been presented for payment, as a check.

overage *Accounting, Finance* The amount that a budget value is exceeded, such as for the expense of a project, or the materials required to produce an order. *Manufacturing* Excess product fabricated, as for a custom order.

overbooked Generally, of a condition in which a hotel, airline, etc. that has accepted reservations for more space than they have available. *Manufacturing* Often expressing a condition in which a manufacturing operation accepts more orders than it can fill in a timely fashion, either because of poor planning or unexpected production delays.

overdraft *Finance* A withdrawal, or attempt to withdraw, from a bank account, an amount in excess of the balance in the account.

overextended Of a business that has expanded its means of production in anticipation of an increase in demand that does not materialize, or one that is caught up in a growing market and expands to accommodate it without properly preparing for additional cash needs. *Finance* A situation in which one has made financial commitments or been allowed credit in excess of the ability to pay.

overflow *Computers* A condition in which the result of

calculations is too large to be accommodated by a program, so that the number is truncated or an error condition is created.

overhead *Accounting* The costs, mostly fixed, that do not relate to a specific product or operation, such as rent, utilities, or administration. *Computers* Volatile memory that is used by various operating and utility functions, and is therefore not available for programs. Of the amount of volatile memory required by an application or utility.

overkill *Colloq.* That which is excessive. *Manufacturing* The extravagant allocation of resources to accomplish a task, resulting in needless extra expense. *Marketing* Excessive promotion of a product that wastes advertising dollars. Excessive claims for a product that may actually reduce sales because the buyer does not consider them believable.

overload *Computers* A condition that can cause a crash, brought on by an attempt to transfer more data than memory can hold, or transferring data faster than the CPU can process it.

overqualified *Labor Relations* Of one who is engaged in, or applying for, a type of work that does not require his or her level of education, experience, or competence. Employers are often reluctant to hire those who are overqualified because of concern that they may not adjust to the drop in status, and that they will leave as soon as more suitable employment becomes available.

overrun *Accounting, Finance* The amount by which a budgeted item exceeds projection, as a *cost overrun*. *Manufacturing* Surplus production beyond that called for in an order and that may not be readily sold or that must be sold at a reduced price.

oversold *Manufacturing* Of production facilities that cannot deliver the amount of goods by the date promised, either because of poor planning or unexpected delays. *Marketing* Of a prospect lavished with too much attention or a product for which extravagant claims are made, either of which may create concern about credibility, and cause a drop in sales.

overtime pay A premium for work beyond the normal daily or weekly hours set by law or contract; most hourly workers are covered by Federal law that decrees a minimum of a 50% premium over base pay for work beyond forty hours in one week, while union contracts often call for fewer regular time hours and a premium of 100% in certain situations.

overvalued *Accounting* Of an asset, such as inventory or a patent that is recorded on the books at a cost that is in excess of its market value.

overwrite *Computers* To save information to storage already occupied, thus obliterating the old data.

owner-operator Of one who owns and manages a business. Often used to describe a truck driver who operates his or her own rig and contracts for work through a service or another carrier.

owners' equity *Finance* The total value of the owners' interest in a business. The net assets of a company.

pack *Computers* The compression of data for more efficient use of disk storage space.

package *Computers* A desktop system that includes a computer, monitor, printer, programs, etc. Two or more programs sold as a unit. *Labor Relations* Descriptive of the aggregate of benefits, wages and fringes, that make up a collective bargaining agreement. *Marketing* The pieces that make up a direct mail packet, taken as a unit.

packaged goods Consumer products packaged for sale by the manufacturer.

packaged software *Computers* A program that is available on the open market, adaptable to a variety of uses.

packing list An accounting of the material contained in a shipment. An inventory of the contents of a package.

padding *Colloq.* Uncalled-for additions, often for personal gain, as in cheating on an expense account. *Marketing* Embellishing the claims for a product in advertising.

page *Computers* A unit of memory used by the computer to manipulate data in storage. A single sheet of output from the printer.

pagination *Computers* The numbering of printed pages in a document or file.

paid-in capital *Finance* Money paid by investors in exchange for stock.

paper *Finance* Generally, notes or other obligations.

paper feeder *Computers* The device that controls the flow of paper through the printer.

parallel *Computers* Descriptive of operations that occur simultaneously.

parallel interface *Computers* A multichannel interface that allows the transfer of a full computer word at one time.

parallel port *Computers* A connection on the computer for communicating with a peripheral device, such as a printer.

parallel processing *Computers* Processing of two or more tasks simultaneously by a computer.

parameter *Computers* A limit or characteristic, as of a program or operating system.

parent company A company that has ownership or control of another company or companies. Ownership of a subsidiary may be incidental to the operation of a parent company, or it may be its only purpose. See also *holding company*.

parse *Computers* To break down into parts, as in separating the elements of a data string from a database into columns for a spreadsheet.

partition *Computers* A divider, as on a disk for file management or for processing a database sort.

partnership *Law, Finance* An organization owned by two or more persons who are individually responsible for the debts of the partnership. See also *limited partnership*.

password *Computers* A series of characters or symbols by which a user gains access to a computer, application or file.

past due *Finance* Of any note or obligation that has not been paid by the due date.

patent *Law* An official public document that grants a special right or privilege; usually, of the exclusive right to manufacture, or to profit from the manufacture, of an invention for a specified period of time.

patent pending Statement issued after a claim for patent is filed so as to serve notice of such filing during the time that a patent search is being conducted to determine whether the invention is indeed unique and patentable according law.

paternalistic Of the nature of a father. Descriptive of a company whose management tends to take a fatherly interest in the employees.

path *Computers* The course followed by the computer in seeking programs and files.

patron One who supports or encourages; a benefactor. In business, a regular client.

pattern recognition *Computers* The technique used by a program to identify elements through comparison with a standard matrix as in optical character recognition.

pay *Accounting* To render to an individual or company, that which is due for goods or services rendered, etc. To discharge a debt or other obligation by reimbursement.

payback, payback period *Accounting, Finance* The time required to recoup the investment in a project. Basically, payback is calculated by dividing the amount of the investment by the amount of money the investment will return each year. Various methods, however, take differing views in calculating the amount of money returned. For example, a simple payback for investment in manufacturing equipment may discount profit on the goods produced during the payback period, considering it as part of the return, whereas a marginal payback may deduct profits, as well as the interest that could be earned on the money invested from the return, thus arriving at a longer payback period.

payee The one to whom a payment is made or to whom a debt is owed.

payer The one pays money owed or is obligated to pay at some time in the future.

payload *Commerce* Any commodity carried by truck, train, airplane, etc. The portion of a cargo that is producing revenue.

payout *Accounting* Any disbursement of funds.

pay period *Accounting* The interval for which salaries or wages are calculated and paid. Customarily, wages are paid daily or weekly, while salaries are often weekly, bi-weekly, semi-monthly, or monthly.

payroll *Accounting* The total paid out by a company for salaries and wages during a given period. The total cost to a company for labor, including amounts paid out to workers, plus deductions for withholding tax, FICA, insurance, pension fund, union dues, etc., and the employer's contribution to FICA, unemployment insurance, medical or retirement benefits, etc.

payroll register *Accounting* A complete record of payroll for all employees, including current and accumulated, regular and overtime hours, sick pay, vacation pay, deductions, etc.

PC, personal computer Generally, a small computer used by a single person, although it may be networked with other computers or file servers. *Personal computer* has been commonly synonymous with *desktop computer*, but new, powerful, laptop and notebook computers are increasingly becoming the machine of choice for a personal computer.

peak Descriptive of the time or period of greatest

activity, such as the primary buying season for a particular product.

pecuniary *Financial* Involving money, as *pecuniary damages* that is monetary compensation for injury.

peddler An itinerant salesperson who deals in a variety of merchandise. *Colloq.* Any salesperson.

penalty *Finance* A charge for the late payment of a debt or other obligation. In some loan or mortgage contracts, or in the absence of a prepayment clause in a loan or mortgage contract, a charge for repaying before the maturity date. A charge for early withdrawal of an investment. *Law* Punishment imposed by a court, as for commission of a crime or a negligent act. That which is forfeited by not exercising a right, as the payment for an option to buy or sell.

pencil pusher *Colloq.* An office worker.

penny stock *Finance* Speculative shares commonly trading for less than one dollar. Generally, a term of disparagement, although some have achieved investment grade over time.

pension fund *Finance* Money accumulated for the payment of pensions to workers after retirement, mostly invested in a number of stocks and bonds, seeking the best return to fill cash needs in the future.

pension plan *Finance* A program established by a company, labor union or other organization that provides income for workers after retirement. Such programs typically are financed to a greater or lesser extent by both employers and employees.

per annum By or for the year; annually.

per capita For each person, such as *per capita income*

that is the total income of a particular group of people, a nation, etc. divided by the number of persons in the group.

perceived value *Marketing* The apparent worth to the observer of a thing regardless of actual material value, as a consumer product. *Perceived value* can be an important element in the pricing of consumer goods, when a small change may make a product more attractive to the buyer, and lead to an increase in sales and profits.

per diem By the day; for each day, as an allowance for expenses.

perfect competition *Finance* A condition in the marketplace wherein no buyer or seller has the power to dominate or significantly influence the price of a product or service.

perfected Amended or modified to the point that further improvement is impossible. In actual use, often an expression of that which has been developed to the point of being satisfactory for the use intended, as a product or a process.

performance Generally, an act or accomplishment. *Law* Fulfillment of an obligation, especially for duty specified by a contract. *Finance* Of the return achieved by an investment. *Manufacturing* Of the quality of operation, such as for employees or equipment.

performance bond *Finance* A third party guarantee of the satisfactory completion of a contract; in the event of default the surety agrees to take over the contract or to pay damages up to the limit of the bond.

period *Accounting* An interval of time between events, as an accounting period of approximately thirty days. The number of intervals into which an event is divided, as twelve accounting periods in the year.

period cost *Accounting* An indirect expense that is linked to time rather than units of production, as utilities, rent, administrative expense, etc.

periodic costing *Accounting* A system of calculating the cost of goods and services by measuring expenses for an accounting period, such as a month, against the number of units processed or delivered during that time. Periodic costing is most effective for measuring the performance of a company, division, or department that produces a standard product that does not vary appreciably from one day to the next.

peripheral *Computers* A device that is connected to a computer and controlled by it.

peripheral program *Computers* A utility; a program that adds to the capabilities of a computer or another program, such as a memory manager or grammar checker.

perjury *Law* Willfully telling a lie while under oath. In some jurisdictions, any false swearing in a legal document.

perk *Colloq.* Perquisite. A privilege, fringe benefit, etc. accorded to one in a particular position in the organization, or for all above a certain level in the hierarchical structure of a company, such as a company car or private office.

permanent financing Long-term debt, such as bonds, or equity financing, as for stock.

permanent memory *Computers* A storage medium, such as a computer disk, that retains its memory when power is off.

permit A license or other document giving permission, as for building, conducting a business, etc.

perpetual inventory A system for recording goods transferred to, and removed from, inventory, with a running total showing the effect of each transaction. Some systems also track goods on order or in process, and those that have been promised or allotted for a purpose, so that in addition to an accounting of goods on hand, the inventory record contains notice of anticipated changes for the near future. Such a system allows for the reordering of goods when the amount in inventory plus the amount on order drops below a certain level. Periodically, the book inventory is confirmed or adjusted by a physical count of the stock on hand.

perquisite See *perk*.

per se *Law* By itself; requiring no further proof to establish existence, as negligence that is clearly a breach of duty, and does not require evidence of the existence of the duty.

person *Law* An individual or corporation that has certain legal rights and obligations.

personal computer See *PC*.

personal injury Damage to an individual, such as invasion of privacy, slander, or bodily harm, in contrast to property damage.

personal liability The exposure, or potential exposure, of all of one's assets to the claims of another, especially for the obligations of a business.

Shareholders in a corporation and limited partners are normally protected, as their exposure is limited to their investment. General partners and owners of an unincorporated business, however, are personally responsible for the debts and other obligations of the company.

personal property *Law* Assets owned that can be moved, in contrast to real property and those attachments to real property that cannot be removed without damage to the property.

personnel Collectively, the individuals employed by an organization; those who make up a company's work force.

personnel administration See *personnel management*.

personnel department The office or unit within an organization that is responsible for the screening, hiring, testing, training, etc. of job candidates as well as other administrative tasks associated with the work force, such as posting notices as required by law or at the direction of management, maintenance of each employee's personnel file, tracking eligibility for benefits and keeping records of participation, filing claims, etc. In addition, the personnel department may be responsible for other programs, such as for safety or health, or the publication of a company newsletter.

personnel management The study and implementation of programs for attracting, screening, training, and retaining good employees of the type and number required by the company.

person-to-person call A telephone call placed to a

particular person; such a call is place through an operator who determines that the person called is on the line before releasing the line to the caller. See also *collect call*.

persuasion *Marketing* The process of influencing people to buy a product or service.

Peter Principle The maxim that "every employee tends to rise to his level of incompetence" first stated by Dr. Lawrence J. Peter.

petition *Law* A formal appeal to a court stating the particulars that are seen as cause for judicial action and containing a request for such action .

petty cash *Accounting* An amount of cash that is usually kept in an office to pay incidental expenses or reimburse employees for out-of-pocket costs.

physical inventory An actual count of materials, supplies, finished goods, etc. that are on hand in a storage area or on the shop floor, often taken to confirm the amount shown by a perpetual inventory system

picketing *Labor Relations* A demonstration by those attempting to publicize a dispute and garner support, often in connection with labor negotiations.

piece work Descriptive of labor performed by an individual whose wage is at least in part determined by the level of output.

piercing the corporate veil *Law* A court action that denies the protection of the corporate entity to certain officers or representatives of a corporation who are held accountable for their actions when, for example, they formed the corporation in order to perpetrate fraud.

piggyback *Commerce* The transporting of truck trailers on rail cars for long distance hauls.

pilferage The stealing of small amounts of goods, as by losses of goods in transit, or the misappropriation of company property by an employee.

PIM, personal information manager *Computers* A utility program that provides a means to record data important to an individual, such as a note pad or address book.

pin feed *Computers* A device that feeds a continuous form through a printer by engaging a series of holes along the edges of the form; same as *tractor feed* or *sprocket feed.*

pirated software *Computers* Programs obtained outside of the normal or legal channels.

pixel *Computers* Picture element; a basic component of a computer graphic.

placement Generally, of the installation or disposition of a person or thing. *Labor Relations* Finding employment for an individual who is out of work. Finding the proper position in a company for a candidate for employment. *Marketing* Securing a specific location for an advertisement, as on a particular page or segment of a publication.

plan B *Colloq.* An often hypothetical alternative to a scheme that is unsuccessful.

planned obsolescence *Manufacturing* Fabricating a product with more emphasis on low cost than on durability. *Marketing* Promoting a newer style of an existing product in hopes of convincing the buyer to disregard utility and discard the older model for a newer one.

plant *Accounting* The assets of a company used in the manufacture of goods. The area that is set aside for manufacturing a product, as distinctive from the office area.

pleading *Law* The statement of facts that establish a cause of action in a court of law.

pledge *Law* The transfer of property as security for a debt or other obligation.

plow back *Colloq.* To return profit to a company as working capital or for the acquisition of assets to support the growth of the organization.

plotter *Computers* A computer peripheral that produces charts or graphs as output.

point *Finance* In the trading of stocks, equal to one dollar. In describing interest rates, such as for a bond or mortgage, equal to one percent.

point-of-purchase *Marketing* Of an advertising display placed in the area where merchandise is sold, as in a store or a store window.

point-of-sale See *point-of-purchase*.

point of sale system *Computers* A computer network that accepts input from remote terminals located at a retailer's cash register and uses the data to perform a variety of tasks such as creating sales reports, updating inventory records, etc.

point and click *Computers* The act of selecting an object by moving the mouse cursor to it, then pressing and releasing the mouse button.

poison pill *Finance* Any strategy by a company targeted for takeover that makes it less attractive to the prospective buyer.

pollution Generally, that which makes impure or

unclean. In industry, usually descriptive of effluence that is a by-product or residue from a manufacturing process and that is contaminating the environment.

Ponzi scheme An illegal program to defraud investors, whereby part of the money paid into the program is used to pay high initial returns in order to attract more money that is partly paid out, etc. until the operator disappears.

port *Computers* Any of the connections to a computer that enable the transfer of data.

portal-to-portal pay Wages that accrue from the time the worker leaves home or shop until he or she returns, often of a worker such as a plumber or electrician who normally travels to the client's site to work.

portfolio *Finance* All of the stock, bonds, and other securities held by a particular individual or institutional investor at one time.

posting *Accounting* The recording of a financial transaction in a journal or ledger.

power of attorney *Law* An instrument in writing that attests to the authority of one to act in the place of another in certain circumstances, as for the sale of property.

power surge *Computers* A sudden increase in line voltage that can interfere with communications and is potentially damaging to the elements of a computer and the data stored. Such damage can usually be avoided by the use of a surge protector.

practical capacity *Manufacturing* The largest volume of product that can be manufactured efficiently

pre-billing

when taking into consideration normal delays as for equipment malfunction, employee absence, etc.

pre-billing *Accounting* The practice of tendering an invoice for goods or services before delivery, that may be normal procedure in certain types of business, or as in the case of a client without approved credit when the seller requests payment in advance for part or all of the invoice. In other cases, a seller may bill in advance of delivery with the agreement of the client in order to protect cash flow, or the client may request invoicing in order to show the payable in the current accounting period, as for a government agency working within a strict budget allocation system. Such billing, when recorded on the company's books as revenue requires offsetting entries for anticipated cost in order to match cost and revenue for the period.

predatory pricing *Marketing* Lower than normal pricing of a product as a device to gain entrance to a market or gain a larger share of the market.

preexisting use *Law* Of a property located in an area for which zoning has changed, but which is exempted from the new regulations to the extent that the property existed for other use prior to the effective date of the new ordinance.

preferred stock *Finance* An equity share in the ownership of a company that has preference over common stock in the payment of dividends and in the distribution of assets in event of dissolution. Preferred stock does not entitle the holder to vote for the members of the board of directors.

premises *Law* A general term for buildings and land

216

whose specific meaning varies with the context in which it is used. In respect to a worker, for example, it may mean anywhere that he or she is sent in the course of performing a job.

premium *Insurance* The amount paid as a lump sum or periodically to keep protection in force. *Marketing* Of the relative quality of a product. A gift, bonus, or reward offered to a prospect as an incentive to buy.

premium pay *Labor Relations* Generally, any addition to the regular wage scale, as overtime pay, shift differential, etc.

prepackaged *Marketing* Of a product that is packed and marked by the manufacturer, often to the retailer's specifications, so that it may be sold to the consumer without opening or altering the package in any way.

prepaid Of that which is paid in advance. *Commerce* Indicating of freight charges that have been paid or are to be paid by the shipper directly to the carrier. Reimbursement for such charges is a matter between buyer and seller.

prepaid expense *Accounting* Of a periodic expense that has been documented in the financial records of the company, whether or not actually paid, and that applies to a future accounting period. Such an expense is carried on the balance sheet as a current asset.

prepayment clause *Finance* A designation in a loan agreement that sets forth the terms for payment prior to the due date of the loan, such as for penalty, computation of interest, etc.

preprocessing *Computers* Configuring data before it is

entered into a program, such as by checking for invalid data, or by converting spreadsheet rows to comma separated values for entering into a database.

presentation Generally, that which is submitted, conferred, or shown. In business, frequently a well-prepared speech accompanied by visuals, intended to sell a product or idea to a large group of people. *Law* Producing a negotiable instrument of debt for acceptance or payment; *presentment*.

present value *Finance* Of the current worth of a sum to be received in the future; the amount of money that would have to be invested at a fixed rate to yield a certain amount within a particular length of time.

presort Of mail that is sorted by zip code and bagged by the mailer, and which is then carried by the postal service at a reduced rate.

press kit A package containing press releases and related material that is generally disseminated to publicize an event.

prestige pricing *Marketing* The practice of increasing the price of a product to a level that engenders or maintains, in the mind of the consumer, the perception of quality. The practice in a retail establishment of stocking only those goods that by their price create a perception of quality.

presumption *Law* The assumption of fact based on the knowledge of other facts.

pretax *Accounting, Finance* Of final amounts, such as profit, that have not be adjusted for taxes.

preventive maintenance *Manufacturing* The practice of, or a system for, regularly servicing equipment that is not malfunctioning in the hope of preventing or delaying malfunction.

price *Commerce* Variously, the amount of money or other consideration asked for something, or the amount for which it is traded. In the case of goods or services offered at a discount, for example, the price quoted as a normal selling price must be the price at which a significant quantity of the goods or services were sold.

price discrimination *Marketing* Offering goods for sale to a merchant at a higher or lower price than that quoted to others in similar circumstances.

priced out of the market *Marketing* Of goods or services that are priced too high to sell in a particular market, often of those that have increased in price over time.

price-earnings ratio *Finance* A comparison of the cost of a share of stock at a given time to the annual proceeds per share for the company.

price fixing Generally, any combination of manufacturers, retailers, or of retailers and manufacturers that serves to interfere with the pricing of goods and services. *Law* Under federal antitrust laws, any conspiracy that interferes with the freedom of merchants and their right to price goods or services according to their best judgment.

prima facie *Law* On its face or at first view, that is, apparent at a glance or not requiring further evidence to prove existence, credibility, etc.

primary market *Market* The geographical location or group of buyers that comprises the main area of sales for a product.

prime rate *Finance* The interest rate that a bank charges its most creditworthy clients. Most interest rates are described in terms of the amount over the prime rate.

principal *Commerce* Any of the main parties to a transaction, as a landlord and tenant. *Finance, Law* An amount of money that is owed or on which interest is paid. *Law* One who has committed or aided in the commission of a crime. One who has directed or allowed another to act as his or her agent.

principle A fundamental doctrine, or truth.

print advertising *Marketing* Any material that promotes a company, product, service, etc. in a periodical, such as a newspaper, magazine, etc.

print buffer *Computers* An area of memory reserved for holding data to be transmitted to the printer, allowing operation in the background while other processing is taking place.

print control character *Computers* Any of the symbols that control the operation or output of the printer, as for line spacing, double width characters, etc.

printed circuit *Computers* A circuit created by applying a conductor to an insulated board.

printer fonts *Computers* Type fonts built into a printer or a printer cartridge.

printout *Computers* The printed result of data processing, such as mailing labels, reports, etc.

priority mail A classification used by the postal service for the sending of parcels by first class mail.

prior period adjustment *Finance* A balance sheet item that corrects an error in reporting for the previous accounting period, entered for the purpose of correcting retained earnings and duly noting that it is not a reflection of activities for the current period.

private brand *Merchandising* A trademark name that is owned by a wholesaler or retail chain and usually sold by no other. Most major food chains have their own line or lines of private brands, also called house brand.

private enterprise See *free enterprise*.

private sector Of the segments of the economy that include households and business, and exclude government.

privatization The process of making private, as by buying back the stock of a public company, or turning over a government enterprise to private interests.

probability The likelihood that a thing will happen.

probation *Labor Relations* A trial period or one of testing, as a trial period for a new employee, or disciplinary period for a permanent employee as a last resort before dismissal.

proceeds *Finance* The net funds received from a sale, investment, business venture, etc.

process A particular means of doing something, or the act of doing something following a prescribed method. *Law* A writ directing appearance or compliance.

processing The act of doing something in a prescribed fashion. *Computers* The manipulation of data by the computer.

procurement The process of buying materials and

product

supplies, hiring workers, etc.

product *Colloq.* Commercial goods collectively, as those from a particular company or industry. *Manufacturing* That which is produced; the output of manufacturing or fabrication.

product class *Commerce* A broad grouping of goods that are used by a particular class of buyer, as *household products* or *industrial products*, or a group of goods designed for similar use that are generally considered to be interchangeable, differing only in brand name, quality, appearance, etc.

product costing *Accounting* The recording and analysis of expenses related to the production of goods so as to establish a manufacturing cost.

product development The evaluation and testing of ideas for the creation of new merchandise or improvements to existing goods.

product differentiation *Marketing* A technique for the promotion and marketing of a product that calls for stressing the way in which it is different from competing products.

product fit *Manufacturing* The way in which the fabrication of a new item adapts to the existing equipment and systems. *Marketing* Placement of new product promotion and sales into that of the line of existing products, for example, whether it is to be merged into a product group, or become an upscale version of an existing item.

production capacity *Manufacturing* Any of a number of criteria for determining the maximum output of an operation or manufacturing plant.

production control *Manufacturing* The process, or the

222

department that implements the process, of scheduling materials, machine time, manpower, etc. for the manufacture of orders on hand in a timely fashion.

production line *Manufacturing* A manufacturing technique that involves a series of contiguous stations, each of which performs a portion of the work required for the manufacture or assembly of a product, or part of a product.

productivity *Manufacturing* Descriptive of the level of the output of a manufacturing operation, production line, or machine relative to a standard.

product liability *Law* The principle in the law of torts that one who manufactures or sells a product is responsible for exercising reasonable care to insure that the product is not only safe to be used as intended, but that there is no other inherent danger in possessing the product and that if a defective product is sold, liability may be incurred when there is harm to the buyer as the result of those defects.

product line *Marketing* A group of items that are similar, such as for hair care or car care, directed toward a particular audience, and manufactured by a single producer or distributor.

product manager *Marketing* One who is responsible for the marketing of a product or a line of similar products for a company. See also ***brand manager***.

product mix *Marketing* Of the variety of items that are sold by a company.

product positioning *Marketing* Strategic placement of a manufactured item in the mind of a potential buyer through advertising, as by stressing quality, price, style, etc.

profession Of a vocation that requires considerable training and intellect, as medicine, law, engineering, etc. Collectively, all of those who pursue any such vocation. *Colloq.* Any occupation.

profit *Accounting* Money left in a business or for distribution to shareholders after all costs and charges have been deducted from sales.

profitability *Accounting* Generally, a measure of earnings in relation to sales or assets. Often a measure of the return on a machine or manufacturing operation.

profit center *Accounting* A segment of a business that produces a profit on its own, as a division or subsidiary, or one that contributes to profit, as a department or machine.

profit margin *Accounting* A ratio of income to sales.

pro forma Literally, according to form. *Accounting, Finance* Financial statements that represent events anticipated, as the start of a new business or major changes in an existing one.

program An orderly procedure for accomplishing something, as an *employee training program. Computers* A set of instructions for the processing of data.

program compatibility *Computers* Descriptive of the ability of programs to work together or to share data.

programmable *Computers* Descriptive of a device whose function can be altered by the user.

programmable function key *Computers* A function key to which a command or series of commands may be assigned.

property

programmable mouse *Computers* A computer mouse that may be assigned commands that are executed by the mouse buttons in conjunction with keyboard keys.

programmer *Computer* One who writes instructions for a computer to accomplish a specific task.

programming language *Computers* A precise system of vocabulary and syntax for writing instructions for the computer; a high level language.

program package *Computers* All of the files and manuals needed to run a particular program. Descriptive of the qualities of a program. A set of applications, as for accounting functions, that make up a program.

projection A prediction or estimate of future results based on experience.

promissory note *Finance* A promise in writing to pay a specified amount by a certain date to a particular party or to the bearer of the note.

promoter One who advocates a cause, or finances and organizes an activity. *Law* One who drafts a plan and sets out to raise the capital to start a corporation.

promotion allowance *Marketing* An agreed amount paid to a merchant or distributor by a manufacturer for advertising or promotion of a product, often in relation to the amount of the product purchased.

prompt *Computers* A cursor; a highlight on the monitor screen that indicates where the next character will be entered. A program query or instruction.

property That which is owned, as real estate, personal goods, etc.

property line The boundary of a plot of real estate.

property rights *Law* The right to ownership and profits from land or other possessions.

property tax Assessment by a municipality on the owners of real estate.

proportional spacing *Computers* In desktop publishing, descriptive of the display of type so that the white space between characters is approximately the same regardless of the width of the character itself.

proprietary software *Computers* Packaged software that is sold with the provision that the seller retains ownership and the buyer purchases only the license to use the software subject to the provisions of a licensing agreement.

proprietorship A business enterprise owned by one person.

pro rata In proportion.

prorate *Accounting* To distribute proportionally, as the allocation of expense to match it with the proper period or revenue.

pros and cons Of the reasons for or against a proposal.

prospect *Marketing* A possible customer; one who may be interested in a particular product.

prospectus Generally, information about an enterprise or institution, often one that is new, describing features, attractions, etc. *Finance, Law* A document disclosing the financial condition of a corporation, required by law to be furnished to each prospective purchaser of the firm's securities.

protected field *Computers* A block of text, formula, etc. in a computer program that cannot be altered, usually user-defined.

protected files *Computers* Read-Only files; computer memory that may be read, but that cannot be altered.

protectionism A policy that advocates restricting the importation of foreign goods in order to protect domestic production.

protocol *Computers* The conventions governing the transfer of data between a computer and peripherals, or another computer.

proviso *Law* A condition, stipulation, or clarification in a contract, statute, etc.

proximate cause *Law* That which directly effects a result and without which such result would not have occurred.

proxy Generally the authority to act for another. *Law, Finance* The empowerment, or one who is empowered, to vote the shares of another at a stockholder's meeting.

proxy statement *Finance* Information that is required by Securities and Exchange Commission regulations to be given to each shareholder prior to corporate elections.

prudence The quality of exercising sound judgment.

prudent man rule *Law* The standard for judging that a trustee who is allowed latitude in investment decisions has acted properly to preserve the principal and seek a reasonable return on investment.

public accountant A licensed accountant who performs professional accounting services for the general public. Licensing requirements are not as stringent as for a certified public account, a designation that is more prestigious; however, the public accountant is qualified to perform most of the same tasks.

public corporation A corporation formed by a political entity for a specific purpose, such as that of a municipality, water district, postal service, etc.

public domain *Law* Comprising all of the lands and waters owned by the United States and the states individually, as distinguished from that owned by individuals or corporations. Of information that may be derived by anyone and that is not subject to copyright.

public interest Generally descriptive of that which is considered not to be disruptive or threatening to the safety of the general public. *Public interest* encompasses a very broad sense of values and is most usually defined by the negative, that is, those things that are *contrary* to public interest, in which context may be placed a broad category of offenses to an individual or to society collectively.

publicity *Marketing* That part of promotion dealing with efforts to make the public take notice of a person, product, company, etc.

public land See *public domain.*

publicly held *Finance* Of a corporation whose shares are owned by a broad range of investors.

public offering *Finance* A proposition for the sale of securities to a broad range of investors.

public policy An official attitude regarding a matter of public interest that may impact on the conduct of business, introduction of legislation, etc.

public record Generally, government documents that

are readily available to the community, such as records of real estate transaction, court actions, etc.

public relations Of the wide dissemination of information intended to cast a favorable light on a person, company, or situation.

public sector *Finance* Of that part of the economy relating to government and governmental bodies, as contrasted to business and households.

public service advertising Free advertising that is directed to the common good, as by government or private welfare agencies promoting health or safety.

public utility A privately owned, government supervised, corporation that sells services to the public, such as for electricity or water.

public works Projects for the benefit of the public, sponsored by a government body, such as the construction of schools or roads.

punitive damages *Law* Payment in addition to compensation for actual losses, levied as a punishment in cases of willful or malicious misconduct.

purchase Generally, to obtain for a price. That which is obtained for a price. *Law* To acquire property in exchange for valuable consideration.

purchase order A document that authorizes a vendor to furnish goods or services as outlined in the document and for an agreed price.

purchasing agent One who is responsible for obtaining materials, supplies, services, etc. that are required in the normal operation of business.

purchasing power The value of money based on the goods and services that it can buy.

pure competition Descriptive of an ideal condition in

which there are many buyers and sellers of a stable product so that none can cause undue influence on the supply or demand; where there is easy access to, and departure from, the market; and there is no collaboration to fix prices, supplies, etc.

pyramiding Generally, the extended use of leverage to promote expansion. *Finance* The use of unrealized profits in an investment to secure financing for purchasing further investments. *Law* Any scheme that attempts to defraud by creating an impression of worth where little or none exists, such as a Ponzi scheme. *Marketing* A marketing plan in which non-exclusive rights to distribute a line of consumer products are sold along with the products.

qualified endorsement *Finance* A signature on the back of a check or other negotiable that transfers the payment to another, or that restricts the condition of payment, such as *for deposit only*.

qualified opinion *Accounting, Finance* An auditor's comment as to any limitation, reservation or exception that is taken to the financial statement, as for the possible effects of pending litigation or tax liability.

qualified prospect *Marketing* An individual or organization that has been identified by lifestyle, need, etc. as a prospective buyer for a particular product. Often used as well to describe one who has the authority and the resources to buy.

quality Any of the distinctive characteristics of a thing, often implying rank or grade.

quality control *Manufacturing* Of the efforts to maintain a grade of product that adheres to a certain

standard, set by company policy, engineering specifications, etc. The responsibility for controlling quality is normally divided between production personnel
and those of an independent department or unit
within the company. Production workers have an
ongoing obligation to monitor the quality of goods as
they are produced, whereas the quality control unit
is often responsible for more detailed testing of in-
coming materials and finished goods, collecting statistical data and reporting on failure rates, etc.

quantity discount *Marketing* A rebate, offered by a
manufacturer, distributor, etc., for the purchase of
multiple units of an item in an attempt to create
additional sales and based on the premise that the
rebate reflects a saving in handling cost.

quarterly Every three months, as a periodic financial
reports, etc.

quasi contract *Law* An informal contract, said to exist when in the normal course of business, a service
that is not specifically contracted is performed in
conjunction with that contracted. When such performance is of clear benefit to the buyer, the seller is
entitled to compensation, such as for the replacement of a worn part that affects the smooth operation of an automobile engine when the buyer
contracted for a tune-up.

query language *Computers* Formal program notation
for requesting specific data, as from a database.

queue *Computers* A list of files or data batches for
processing, such as those to be printed out.

quick assets *Finance* Cash and those assets that can
be readily turned into cash such as accounts

receivable, or marketable securities.

quick ratio *Finance* A comparison of quick assets with current liabilities, a measure of an organization's ability to quickly liquidate current liabilities.

quid pro quo *Law* Literally, what for what, or the giving of something for something. Consideration, as that which each party to a contract is given in return for that which each gives.

quitclaim deed A document the relinquishes ones claim to a property without acknowledging that such a claim ever existed. A quitclaim deed, therefore, does not convey clear title.

quota Generally, an amount or share that is assigned. *Manufacturing* The number of units of production expected from a manufacturing operation, an assembly line, a group of workers, a machine, etc. *Marketing* The number or value of units expected to be sold by an individual, in a particular market, or in total during a given period. In a time of shortage, the number of units allocated to each client or to a particular market.

quotation A statement of the price at which an item or group of items is offered for sale. Response to an inquiry that may be a simple statement of price or one that includes a detailed description of the item or items.

QWERTY keyboard *Computers* A keyboard with letters arranged the same as those on a typewriter.

racket *Colloq.* Any dishonest practice. Often, any means of earning money with relative ease. *Law* Obtaining money illegally, as by extortion or fraud; *racketeering*.

rack jobber *Marketing* A wholesaler who sells a variety of convenience merchandise and who maintains the display for such merchandise in the customer's store or outlet.

raider *Finance* A person or corporation who threatens to take control of a company by a controlling interest in its stock.

RAM, Random Access Memory *Computers* Very fast memory that can be accessed independent of the previous access. Such memory is used to temporarily hold the programs and data being processed; such memory is lost when the computer is shut down.

random sampling *Manufacturing* Selection of a number of items in which each choice is independent of all previous choices, that is, there is no pattern to the selection. A system of random sampling is normally used for quality control testing on the theory that a regularly placed sample, such as the first of each batch of one hundred, or regularly timed, as selected at a certain time of the day, is more likely to exhibit a pattern of defects that does not mirror the pattern one might find if all were inspected.

range *Computers* All of the values that a variable may assume. In a spreadsheet or database, user-defined limits of data affected by a command.

rank and file Generally, blue collar workers, or employees who are not a part of management. *Labor Relations* The dues paying member of a union.

rate card *Marketing* A schedule of media rates showing cost for single insertion, discounts for multiple insertion, etc. and other information pertinent to placing an ad, such as mechanical requirements, etc.

rate of return See *return on investment*

rat race *Colloq.* Of the level of activity and stress involved in building a career or just making a living, often disparagingly, as of rats racing on a wheel and going nowhere.

raw data *Computer, Marketing* Descriptive of information that has been collected, but that has not been catalogued or analyzed.

raw material *Accounting, Manufacturing* Ingredients, components, or goods that are to be converted to a finished product.

read-only *Computers* Of a file or other section of memory that can be accessed, but not changed.

read/write head *Computers* The device in a disk drive that reads from and writes to the storage disk.

real estate *Finance, Law* Land and anything fixed to the surface, as a building, fence, trees, etc., and that which is beneath, as minerals, or above.

real property Same as real estate.

realtor One who acts as agent for those who wish to buy or sell real estate.

reasonable *Law* A subjective quality by which actions are often judged, especially in cases of tort liability, as for *reasonable care*, that is the caution expected of one in a particular set of circumstances, or of a *reasonable person*, that is one who exercises a measure of intelligence and judgment required by society for protection of their common interests.

rebate *Marketing* An amount refunded or deducted from an invoice for goods or services as a reward for a volume purchase, reimbursement for promotional expense, etc. Occasionally, an illegal kickback.

recall The calling back of a faulty product for refund, replacement, or repair by a manufacturer, sometimes ordered by a government agency when public safety is a consideration.

receipt *Commerce* A document drawn by a seller or shipper, with copies for the buyer or receiver, that attests to payment or delivery or both.

receivables *Accounting* The aggregate of all the claims for payment due a company.

receiver *Finance, Law* One who is appointed by a court to oversee and preserve property that is the subject of litigation, usually insolvency. In such cases, the receiver takes possession, but not title, of the entity and manages its affairs as a going concern pending final disposition.

receiving record *Commerce* A document, register, or account of goods delivered to a warehouse, retail store, manufacturing plant, etc. In some instances, a document is prepared with detailed information about each shipment received; in others, a single document contains a list of a shipments received for the day with any variances noted on the shipping papers, that are attached as the source documents. In all cases, receiving records are used to verify invoices as they are received.

reciprocity An exchange for mutual benefit. *Commerce* Often, an informal agreement whereby two or more companies offer mutual courtesy, as by each selling their products to the other.

reclamation *Manufacturing* The process of making or

recovering useful products from waste, such as by processing used photographic film to recover the silver. See also *recycling*.

reconciliation *Accounting* A balancing, so as to bring into agreement, such as for ledger accounts or a bank statement.

record Any documenting of a transaction; the transaction so documented. *Accounting* To make an entry into the journals or ledgers of a company. *Computers* A unique set of information in a database. See also *field*.

recoup To regain something or an equivalent, as the amount of an investment, or of a loss. *Law* To hold back a portion, or reduce the amount, of a claim with valid reason for doing so, such as proof of an earlier payment against the claim.

recourse *Finance, Law* The right to pursue a judgment that is not limited to the property held as security, against one who defaults on a debt.

recovery *Accounting* The residual value of an asset after it has been fully depreciated. The recouping of overhead expense by allocation to various profit centers. *Law* The establishment of a due and just debt by action of a court.

recruitment *Labor Relations* The process of attracting, screening, and hiring personnel.

recycling Reprocessing that which is considered waste to make it into a usable product, most common for plastic, paper and glass that are recycled for use in making special grades of the same product. See also *reclamation*.

redlining *Finance, Law* Illegal discrimination against

borrowers living in certain neighborhoods.

red tape *Colloq.* Of the elaborate procedures or forms required to accomplish a task, often through a government agency.

reference check *Labor Relations* The process of verifying the information on an employment application as to places of previous employment, time of employment, reason for leaving, etc. as well as to learn as much as possible about the applicant.

referral Generally, the directing of information to another. Often a recommendation, as for employment, use of a product, etc.

refinance *Finance* To restructure debt or obligations to better suit a person or company's needs, as by extending the term, increasing the principal, etc.

reformat *Computers* To change the style of a body of text, as by altering margins, type face, etc. To convert a file for use by a different application.

refresh *Computers* To revive or renew volatile memory so as to maintain or record changes, such as by redrawing the image on the monitor screen.

refund *Finance* To refinance an obligation, usually to save interest charges. *Marketing* To reimburse a buyer for returned merchandise, or for a promotional rebate.

refusal *Commerce, Law* The right of a buyer to reject that which is furnished under a contractual agreement.

registered check *Finance* A check issued by a bank for a client who sets aside funds in the amount of the check.

registered mail Mail that may be insured, and that is

signed for by each postal employee handling it and
by the recipient, verification of delivery furnished by
the postal service. See also *certified mail*.

regulated industry A business that is subject to government oversight, such as a local utility that is restricted as to the amount of profit it can make and
that must seek approval for rate increases.

regulation An ordinance, statute, or law that governs
or controls conduct.

regulatory agency A governmental body, acting in the
public interest, responsible for the supervision or
restraint of an activity.

relational database *Computers* A database that is associated with another, usually be a common field, so
that information may be drawn from both and combined in a report.

relational operator *Computers* That which associates
two entities, as a common field in a database. A
mathematical symbol that represents the relationship between two values, such as > (greater than), <
(less than), = (equal to), etc.

release *Finance* Being freed from an obligation, as by
discharging a debt; a document that is proof of such
discharge. *Law* The giving up of a right or claim, by
action or a written instrument, such as permission
by the owner of a copyrighted work that allows quotation or use of such a work.

reliability Of the quality of a thing to do that which is
expected of it or for which it is intended. *Accounting*
Of the confidence level of an auditor that financial
records and accounting procedures are in accordance with accepted practice. *Finance* Of the extent

to which financial reports are free of error or bias. *Marketing* In direct mail marketing, the ability of a particular mailing list or package to garner the anticipated level of return. In advertising, emphasis on the durability of a product.

remainder Generally, that which is left. *Commerce* Of a dealer who specializes the buying of excess product for resale at greatly reduced prices to other dealers or directly to the consumer, called *remaindering*.

remedy *Law* The means by which a court attempts to right, or compensate for, a wrong.

remit *Finance* To pay, as to satisfy a debt. *Law* To submit a matter for consideration.

remote *Computers* Descriptive of a terminal, data collection point, computer, or peripheral that is not in the immediate area of the host computer.

remote access *Computers* Connecting, as by modem over telephone lines, and interacting, with a computer or peripheral that is at a distance.

remote entry system *Computers* A data entry terminal that is located at a significant distance from the host computer.

remuneration *Labor Relations* Any pay or compensation for work performed, whether direct, as wages, or indirect, as fringe benefits.

renege To fail to honor an agreement or promise.

renegotiate To reopen a contract in hope of reaching agreement on more favorable terms. *Labor Relations* To revise the terms of a labor agreement in accordance with a reopener provision in contrast to establishing a new contract, usually because of changing conditions or the passage of time.

renewable resource Of a natural resource that replaces over time if properly managed, such as a forest.

renewal option A right to keep a contract in force if certain options are met.

rent Payment for the use of property. Income or profit earned from the ownership of land.

rent control Local regulations that establish a maximum rent that may be charged for certain dwellings, or the maximum increase allowed from one lease period to another.

reopener provision *Labor Relations* A clause in a collective bargaining agreement that allows either party to exercise the right to renegotiate certain parts of the contract before its expiration, usually if certain conditions are met, such as an excessive increase in the Consumer Price Index.

reorder point In a system for inventory control, the level established for placing an order to restock.

reorganization Generally, a change in the structure of an organization, such as financial, or by revising the lines of authority and responsibility so as to improve performance. *Finance* The restructuring of a company after filing for bankruptcy, while it works out a plan for repayment of outstanding debt. *Law* The restructuring of a firm as by merger, acquisition, consolidation, etc.

rep *Colloq.* A representative, as for sales or customer service.

repairs and maintenance *Accounting* An expense item for the work required to maintain property in useful condition without extending its life.

repeat sales *Marketing* Of the tendency of buyers to reorder a product by brand name, an important factor in successful advertising and marketing.

replacement cost *Accounting* Price of a comparable asset in the current market; same as current cost. *Insurance* A provision in some policies that provides protection up to the replacement cost of an asset regardless of original cost or book value.

report Generally, an accounting or summarizing of data; the data so summarized; presentation, orally or written, of organized data. *Computers* A document on disk, or a hard copy that summarizes the output from data processing.

repossession *Law* The reclaiming of a possession by the seller for non-payment.

representation *Marketing* Claims made for a product in advertising.

repudiation *Law* The statement of refusal to fulfill a duty or obligation as required by contract. Such refusal is not a breach unless the other party to the contract treats it as such and sues for damages.

requisition In business, a formal request for supplies or materials; the document used to request such materials.

resale value *Accounting* The price that an asset would bring if offered for sale, in contrast to or residual value.

rescission *Law* The act of canceling a contract and return of the parties to their condition prior to the making of the contract, as by agreement of the parties to the contract, by their actions, or by court decree.

research A systematic investigation and analysis of the data compiled about a specific subject, such as for a new process, the market for a product, etc.

reserved word, reserved symbol *Computers* A word or symbol in a programming language that has a special meaning.

reserve for bad debts *Accounting* An amount set aside for anticipated bad debts, credits, etc., usually as a percentage of *sales*. A reasonable reserve for bad debts serves to reduce profits and, for reporting purposes, to represent more accurately the financial position of a company.

residual value *Accounting* The value of an asset after accumulated depreciation has been deducted; the book value, as distinct from actual cost or market value. The scrap value of an asset, deducted before calculating depreciation.

resolution A formal statement of intent or opinion, often formulated by a group, as a board of directors, a committee, union group, etc. *Computers* Of the fineness of the detail of an image as on a monitor screen or output from a printer.

resources All that is available for use, especially to accomplish a task, such as the personnel and equipment available to a manufacturer. *Computers* the sum of all the capabilities of a computer system determined by its hardware and software configuration.

resource allocation The appropriation of personnel, money, equipment, etc. for the accomplishment of a product. Often a designation of the assignment of limited resources to the accomplishment of a variety of tasks according to importance.

restitution *Law* The act of correcting a wrong by attempting to restore the conditions that existed before the wrong was committed; payment to an injured party to correct a wrong; or payment by a party that committed a wrong in order to prevent unjust enrichment to that party.

restraint of trade *Law* Any act or agreement that tends to restrict free competition, as by price fixing, allocation of a market among suppliers, etc., and that operates to the detriment of buyers of goods or services.

restrictive covenant *Law* A stipulation in a real estate contract that places limits on the way in which land may be used or of the type of building that may be built thereon, etc.

retail *Marketing* Of the sale of goods in small quantities directly to the consumer.

retail display allowance *Marketing* A payment or rebate offered by a manufacturer to a retailer in consideration for improved positioning of the manufacturer's product on the retailer's shelves.

retained earnings *Accounting, Finance* Part of shareholder's equity representing accumulated profits that have been kept in the business. A balance sheet account for recording such equity.

retainer *Law* A fee paid to insure availability of services, as an advance payment to a professional, such as an attorney, to insure his or her availability for consultation from time to time, or commitment to take on a particular lawsuit.

retirement plan Any strategy for assuring continued

income after retiring from a job or career; usually, a program sponsored by an employer for the employees of the company.

retroactive Descriptive of that having effect on something that occurred prior to its existence or enactment, as a *retroactive pay increase* in a collective bargaining agreement that stipulates an increase in wages that is to take affect in the past and therefore requires adjustment of all wages paid since that time.

return *Finance* Of the income or profit from an investment or the sale of merchandise. *Marketing* The exchange of goods for like merchandise or a refund. The amount of response to a direct mail marketing campaign.

return on investment, ROI *Finance* The income expected to be realized from any investment, regardless of size, made by the company in plant facilities, equipment, etc. expressed as a percentage of the investment. In many companies, return on investment is the primary yardstick by which investment decisions are made and by which the performance of a manager is measured.

revenue Income, as from particular source, or collectively.

reversal A change of fortune, such as a drop in sales or income. *Law* The setting aside, or vacating, by a court, of a judgment of a lower court.

reverse discrimination *Labor, Law* The exclusion of a particular race or class of people in order to provide employment to those who have traditionally been the target of discrimination.

reversing entry *Accounting* The entry that zeroes out an account, literally reversing the total of the entries for a prior period, in order to begin recording data for the new period.

reverse video *Computers* The display, on a monitor screen, of dark characters on a light background.

revocable trust *Finance* An agreement for deeding property to another, while receiving income from the property.

revolving credit *Finance* An agreement whereby a client may borrow up to a set limit, often requiring periodic payments against the outstanding balance, and allowing additional borrowing as the balance is reduced.

rider *Insurance* An addition to an insurance policy that supplements or in some way modifies coverage of the basic policy.

right of action *Law* The right to bring suit in a court of law, as to protect a right or correct a wrong. See also *cause of action.*

right of refusal A privilege granted by agreement, or for consideration, that gives one an opportunity to buy or bid on something before all others, or to meet any other bid. Also called *right of first refusal.*

right of rescission *Law* The privilege of a buyer to cancel a credit contract, without penalty, within three working days from that of the signing of the contract.

right of survivorship *Finance* A type of ownership that provides for the transfer of a decedent's interest in jointly held property to the survivor. See also *joint tenancy, tenancy in common.*

right to work *Labor Relations, Law* Of the state laws that make illegal any stipulation in a collective bargaining agreement that requires membership in a union as a condition for securing or continuing employment. See also *closed shop, open shop, union shop*.

risk management *Finance* Procedures to protect assets of a business or its potential for future profit against possible losses or to minimize losses if they occur, especially in reference to a specific venture or undertaking.

robotics *Manufacturing* The science that deals with the study, design, fabrication, and application of machines to perform certain repetitive or dangerous tasks that would otherwise have to be performed by human labor.

ROI See *return on investment*.

role playing *Labor Relations* A technique used in training or human relations in which participants portray and act out the part of others in order to recognize their own reactions to a situation, to better understand why others act as they do, and to learn the appropriate behavior for such situation.

rolling stock *Commerce* Carriers of freight, as truck trailers, rail cars, etc., generally, collectively, of all such conveyances owned by a particular company.

ROM, read-only memory *Computers* Of permanent memory, such as that stored on a compact disk, that can be accessed to be used by the computer or viewed by the operator, but that cannot be altered in any way.

root directory *Computers* The primary directory in a

hierarchical file structure containing the command and system configuration files.

routine *Computers* A set of computer instructions that performs a particular task.

routing *Commerce* The means by which goods will be conveyed from place to place, as by truck or rail, by a particular carrier, or by a specific route.

royalty *Commerce, Law* An amount charged or paid for the use of a property owned by another, such as for an invention or literary work. Such royalty may be a lump sum payment, an amount per unit, or a percentage of revenue, and may be limited as to quantity, time, exclusivity, etc.

rubber check *Colloq., Finance* A check that is no good, that is, one drawn on an account that does not contain sufficient funds to cover it.

run *Commerce* Of a particular batch of merchandise, often, presumed to have all been fabricated during the same period. *Computer* Of the operation of a program or the processing of data. One pass through a set of data to be processed. *Manufacturing* Of the quantity of goods to be produced at one time or in series.

running cost *Accounting* The cost of operating a machine or production line, including direct labor and direct overhead, usually related to units produced or hours of operation.

run time *Computers* The interval required for a computer to perform a specific task or series of tasks, such as a mail merge. *Manufacturing* The period required to machine one unit of production, or a number of units that comprise a particular job or production lot.

sack *Colloq.* To dismiss, as an employee.

salary Compensation, at fixed intervals, such as weekly, monthly, etc. for services rendered, especially for those working in a clerical or professional capacity.

sale *Law* An agreement or contract for the transfer of a product or service from seller to buyer for a specified amount of money.

sales analysis *Marketing* The compilation and study of sales by product, region, profitability, etc. so as to determine the means to generate the most profit from a company's advertising and sales efforts.

sales budget A projection of anticipated sales for all of a company's products during a number of fixed periods in the future by product or product type, so as to anticipate needs in terms of workers, cash flow, etc.

sales contract A formal agreement between buyer and seller as to the terms and conditions of a sale.

sales forecast A salesperson's projection of anticipated sales for some period in the future, such as for a month or a year.

sales incentive Any device used to encourage buying or selling, as a premium or special price offered to buyers, or an extra commission, bonus, prize, etc. offered to members of the sales force.

sales pitch *Colloq.* sales presentation.

sales presentation A formal demonstration by a salesperson to a prospective buyer, explaining the benefits, qualities, etc. of a particular product or service and ending with a request for an order.

sales promotion *Marketing* The office or function for encouraging the buying and selling of certain goods and services through special programs. A program designed to increase the sales of a product or service, by motivating salespersons, distributors, prospects, etc.

sales quota The amount of a product, in units or dollars, that a salesperson is expected to sell during a given period.

salvage value *Accounting* The value of an asset after it has been fully depreciated; *scrap value.*

sampling *Manufacturing* The random taking of product from an assembly line or manufacturing unit for testing. The testing of random samples. *Marketing* Testing of a product by a panel of consumers to get their reaction and suggestions. Offering small packages of a product to consumers in hopes of inducing them to buy more.

saturation *Manufacturing* Of a condition in which no additional units of product can be manufactured without increasing investment. *Marketing* Of a condition in there is no longer a market for a product because all prospective buyers own the product. Sometimes used to describe a condition in which satisfactory coverage of a market is achieved, that is, every possible distributor carries the product.

scalable font *Computers* Descriptive of a type font that a computer program can reproduce in a wide range of sizes.

scale *Labor* Of a wage that is the normal rate paid for that particular position.

scanner *Computers,* Of an optical device that reads

and records images for processing by a computer. *Marketing* Of a device that reads markings on a product or product label for recording of a sale, inventory, etc.

schedule A projected or planned sequence of events. *Manufacturing* A projection of the timing of events in the manufacture of a product, such as dates for receipt of materials or parts, start of fabrication, shipping date, etc.

scrap value *Accounting* The value of an asset after it has been fully depreciated; *salvage value.*

screen *Computers* The area on a monitor that displays information from the computer.

screen blanker *Computers* A program that prevents burning an image into a monitor screen by blacking it out after a specified period of inactivity.

screen refresh *Computers* Constant renewal of the monitor screen to provide an image that does not flicker.

screen saver *Computers* A screen blanker that displays a random, moving pattern on the screen.

scrolling *Computers* Movement of the image on a monitor screen to view elements outside its borders.

sealed bid *Commerce* An offer by a vendor that must be sealed when tendered and not disclosed until all bids from all vendors participating in the bidding are opened at a set time and place. A system used by the federal, state and local governments, and public utilities, to insure that the selection process is honest and impartial; bids are publicly opened and recorded, with contracts awarded to the lowest priced qualified bidder.

search *Computers* A feature in some programs that locates a word or phrase in text files, records in a data base file, or a particular file.

search firm A company that specializes in locating key personnel for prospective employers.

seasonal discount *Marketing* The tendency of certain products or services to drop in price during the off season, such as for clothing or a resort hotel.

seasonal employee One who is employed only for a certain time of the year to match increased needs or demand during that period, as a sales clerk during the Christmas shopping period.

seasonal fluctuation Regular variation in the level of activity for a business during certain seasons.

secondary boycott *Labor Relations* The practice of placing pressure on a business to cease its trading with another business that is the source of a grievance.

second mortgage *Finance* The pledging of a property that is already mortgaged. In case of default, the holder of the first mortgage has precedence for claim against default.

secured creditor *Finance* A creditor who is protected against loss by the pledge or assets.

secured debt *Finance* Indebtedness that is guaranteed by a pledge of assets.

securities *Finance* Written instruments that are evidence of a right to a share in money, property, income, etc.

securities analyst *Finance* One who makes a study of a company or an industry in order to assess the worth of investments.

security

security *Finance* Anything that is pledged as surety for the repayment of a loan.

security agreement *Commerce* An agreement between buyer and seller that attests to the seller's retention of interest in that which is sold until the buyer has paid for it.

seed money *Finance* Initial capital raised to start a company or venture.

selective distribution *Marketing* The selling of a product in a restricted market, often because the product is fragile and does not ship well, or only to certain dealers who agree to conform to the manufacturer's standards for promotion, pricing, etc.

self-employed Of one who works at his or her own business.

self liquidator *Marketing* Descriptive of a premium offered, or that can be offered at a price that completely covers the cost and distribution of the item.

self mailer *Marketing* A direct mail package that is self-contained, that is it does not require a separate outer envelope to carry it.

self-service *Marketing* Descriptive of a retail outlet in which the buyer performs most of the functions that would otherwise be provided by store personnel.

seller's market *Marketing* Descriptive of a condition in which there is a shortage of merchandise, excess demand, or few sellers, often marked by high prices and profits.

selling cost *Accounting* The cost of advertising and promotion to attract the interest of potential buyers of a retail product. Frequently, the cost of maintaining a sales force, including salaries, commissions,

252

travel and entertainment expenses, etc., for a company that sells to manufacturers or distributors.

semiannual Twice a year; descriptive of that which occurs every six months.

semimonthly Twice a month, often of a pay period.

semi-variable cost *Accounting* Cost, such as floor supervision, that may vary with the level of production, but not directly with the number of units produced

seniority Of time on a job or the ranking of employees in terms of the amount of time in service to a particular company or on a particular job. Of the priority or privilege extended to one based on length of service. For example, those of greater seniority are often allowed to state their preference of job or shift assignment, and insofar as possible, are given those assignments over one of lesser seniority.

sequential Ordered; one after another. *Computers* Descriptive of data, files, etc. arranged or accessed in a particular order.

sequential search *Computers* A system for locating data that involves an ordered progression through data or files until the search object is found.

serial interface *Computers* A single line connector that transmits data sequentially, one bit a time.

serial port *Computers* A connection on the computer for communicating with a peripheral device.

server *Computers* A computer that stores and manages programs and data for other computers or terminals in a network.

service Generally, of that which one does that is of benefit to another. *Commerce* Descriptive of a company that deals in acts of assistance to another company or for an individual, as for consulting, cleaning, etc. *Labor Relations* Of the length of time an individual has been employed by a company. See also *seniority*.

service charge A fee for things done, often in conjunction with other costs, as that of packaging or shipping a product, maintaining a record of transactions, etc.

service department A designated group or section in a company that performs tasks for the buyer, such as wrapping packages, repairing appliances, etc.; or for other departments in the company, such as equipment repair and maintenance, cleaning, etc.

setback A problem or reversal in a business, a project, etc. that temporarily slows or halts forward progress. The amount by which the boundaries of a building fall short of the property line, often a minimum set by local ordinance. A type of architecture in which each floor or certain floors fall short of the boundary of the floor below, creating a stair step arrangement.

settle Generally, to satisfy an obligation. *Finance* To pay off an outstanding loan. *Law* To resolve a dispute without litigation.

settlement *Law* Generally, the resolution of a matter without going to court.

setup *Manufacturing* The time required to make an assembly line or machine ready to run, or begin fabrication of a particular product.

severance *Labor Relations* Dismissal from a job. Pay given to an employee who has been dismissed, implying that the dismissal was without prejudice or not the fault of the employee.

sexual differential *Labor Relations* A variance in a rate of pay that has no basis except the sex of the recipient, generally against the law although subtle differences in job description or title allow it to continue in some instances.

sexual harassment *Labor Relations* Unwelcome verbal or physical advances of a sexual nature, often by a superior, so that the harassment is intimidating as well.

shakeup *Colloq.* Descriptive of a condition within a company or department marked by significant change in personnel or procedures.

share Generally, a portion of something. *Finance* A vested interest in a company or enterprise, as a share of stock.

shared resources *Computers* Descriptive of a situation in which devices or peripherals serve two or more computers or terminals.

shareholder *Finance* One who owns shares, or has an interest in an enterprise.

shareware *Computers* Non-commercial software, usually available on a trial basis.

shell corporation *Finance* A company that is incorporated with no significant assets or apparent business purpose, often a corporation formed prior to establishing a business plan and raising capital, or to mask fraudulent activities.

shift differential Compensation to an employee over base pay for working what are considered to be less desirable hours, the second or third shift.

shrink pack A thin plastic wrap that adheres tightly

to the product it contains, often mounted on a rigid backing, less expensive than blister pack to produce.

shop floor collection *Accounting, Computers* A system for tracking employee time and production cost from data entered by the employee directly to a station located on the shop floor. Some systems require detailed entry by the employee, while others record time automatically and read a bar code on the employee's time card and on the work order.

shop steward *Labor Relations* A union representative, usually a part of, and elected by, the members of the group of workers that he or she serves, and who is responsible for handling grievances, collecting dues, and conducting other union business on company property and often, company time.

shortcut key *Computers* A combination of a character or function key with a shift key, used to quickly execute a command or series of commands.

shortfall Generally, any deficiency or result that does not meet expectations or needs. *Accounting* An amount of cash received that is less than expected or less than that needed to meet expenses for a given period. *Marketing* Periodic sales that do not meet expectations.

short term *Accounting* Of a period less than one year, or that which is due to be converted in less than one year, as *short term assets* that include *receivables* for which payment is expected, or *short term liabilities* that include *loans* that are due within the year.

shrinkage Usually of inventory that is less than the amount recorded by the inventory control system, often as a result of pilferage, recording errors, or errors in count when issuing supplies.

shutdown *Manufacturing* Cessation of operations due to a lack of orders, materials, workers, etc.

sick leave *Labor Relations* Time allowed for absence caused by illness, often with pay, set by company policy or the terms of a collective bargaining agreement. Extended leave granted in unusual circumstances to an employee who faces a long recuperation period, often without pay, but containing the implied promise of a job on return.

silent partner *Colloq.* Informal description of one who has no investment in a business, but who has been, or continues to be, of great service, as by offering information or advice, garnering prospects, etc. *Finance* One who has invested in, or loaned money to, a business, and who takes no active part in the running of the business; general partner.

simple interest *Finance* Interest that is calculated only on the principal or amount borrowed, in contrast to compounded interest that is applied to the principal plus any accumulated interest charges.

simultaneous processing *Computers* The processing, by a computer, of two or more tasks at the same time.

site audit *Finance* An examination of financial records that is conducted at the offices of the company being examined.

slander *Law* A statement to another that defames the character or reputation of a third party. See also *libel*.

slot *Computers* A position in a computer frame designed to hold a controller board.

slowdown A deliberate or incidental retarding of progress, as a job action by workers who proceed in a deliberate, methodical fashion so as to reduce output, or of the downturn of a business cycle.

slump A sudden, sharp decline in business activity.

small business Generally, of a business that employs less than 100 workers.

small claims court *Law* An informal court for hearing cases involving relatively minor claims, usually for $500 or less.

social contract A general concept of the relationship between persons and entities which holds that all have an obligation to respect the rights of the other.

social security Of the programs under the jurisdiction of the federal government that provide benefits for retirement, disability, unemployment, etc.

soft goods Nondurable goods such as textiles.

soft market *Finance* Of the slow movement in the trading of certain securities. *Marketing* Of a temporary decline in the demand for a product.

soft sell *Marketing* Direct selling or advertising that extols the value of a product, or equates the product with a better lifestyle, romance, etc. and leaves the buyer to make a decision on his or her own. A sales message that follows the old salesman's admonition of *be bright, be brief, and be gone.*

software *Computers* Any program, such as an application, system file, device driver, etc. that furnishes instructions to the computer.

software documentation *Computers* Instructions to the user for the loading and operation of software.

software utilities *Computers* Programs that assist in

the operation of the computer as by improving performance, managing files, etc.

sole proprietorship A business that is owned by one person who has unlimited liability for the debts of the business.

solvency *Finance* Of the ability of a company to meet its obligations as they become due.

sort *Computers* To place data or files in a predetermined order, as alphabetical, by number, by date, by size, etc.

sort field *Computers* In a database file, the field on which the sort is based.

sound driver *Computers* The program that controls the recording, manipulation and reproduction of sound in a multimedia computer.

source data *Computers* Data that has been entered into the computer for manipulation.

source documents *Accounting* Hard copies of orders, sales tickets, invoices, etc. that are the backup for journal entries. *Computers* Any reference that is the basis for data entered into the computer.

space *Accounting* Of the square footage of a plant or department that is the basis for allocating overhead expenses. *Marketing* Of advertising in publications that is priced according to the square inches of space or portion of that is contracted.

special order *Manufacturing* A request for the fabrication of a product that is to be manufactured to the buyer's specifications.

specialty advertising *Marketing* Generally, a reference to promoting a company or product with the use of small gifts that are imprinted with the name of a manufacturer or brand, such as on pens, coffee cups, paperweights, etc.

specialty shop A retail establishment that sells products geared to a particular use or consumer.

specifications *Manufacturing* A written record of an order, containing a complete description of the work to be done, materials required, etc.

speculation *Finance* Investment in an enterprise in the hope of making a profit.

speech recognition *Computers* Of the ability of a computer to accept and act on voice commands.

speech synthesis *Computers* The emulation of the human voice by a computer.

speed key *Computers* A combination of a character or function key with a shift key, used to execute a command or a series of commands.

spell checker *Computers* A feature of some word processing programs that provides verification of spelling in documents.

spike *Colloq.* A momentary sharp increase in electrical current that may damage electronic equipment, especially a computer or its memory. *Computers* A program feature that permits a number of independent elements to be removed from a document to be inserted elsewhere as a unit.

spin-off *Finance* An action that separates a division of a corporation to form a private company.

split See *stock split*.

split screen *Computers* A program feature that permits viewing different sets of data on the monitor screen at the same time.

split shift *Labor* Of a daily work schedule divided into two distinct parts with several hours of unpaid time between them.

spokesperson One who speaks for an entity, by way of press releases, product endorsements, etc.

spooler *Computers* A hardware device, or software, that transfers and stores computer output, such as data to be printed, for processing at a later time.

spot advertising *Marketing* Advertising, usually in broadcast media, that is limited to certain stations, times, etc. in contrast to network advertising.

spot check *Manufacturing* A random sampling of product from a machine or assembly line to confirm that quality requirements are being met.

spreadsheet *Accounting* Data that is arranged in a table or rows and columns, as for a financial report that compares results for several periods. *Computers* A program that aids in the preparation of reports by allowing automatic calculation, linking so that all amounts affected by the change or a single value are updated when that value is changed, etc.

sprocket feed *Computers* A device on a printer that feeds a continuous form through the printer by engaging a series of holes along the edges of the form; same as *pin feed* or *tractor feed*.

stack *Computers* An area of memory in RAM reserved for temporary storage of data.

staff Sometimes, collectively, all of the workers in a company. Often used to designate only those who support the workers in line positions, such as clerks or schedulers who are not directly involved in the production of goods or services.

stake *Colloq.* Of the amount one has invested in a

company or enterprise. Often, a reference to one's portion of the total investment.

standard *Accounting* Of costs, as for materials, labor, etc., that conform to expectations or experience. *Manufacturing* The criterion for quality and quantity by which the performance of a machine, assembly line or crew is measured. Descriptive of material or a product that is fabricated to a usual set of specifications.

standard industrial classification A numbering system used by the federal government to identify and catalogue companies by the type of product or service which they provide.

standardization *Manufacturing* The adoption of specifications for size, quality, etc. that allow the interchanging of certain parts in different products, or the furnishing of raw materials and parts by different suppliers.

standing order *Marketing* A request by a buyer for the periodic delivery of a specified quantity of product at an agreed price unless otherwise instructed.

startup costs *Accounting, Finance* The cost to set up and begin operating a business.

statement *Accounting* A summary of transactions, as for a customer's purchases and payments in the course of a month. *Computer* A line in a program that comprises a single instruction. *Finance* A report of a company's financial transactions, as a cash flow statement.

statistical analysis The evaluation of a body of numerical data relating to a particular subject.

statistical sampling The process of selecting

elements of data to be analyzed.

stats, statistics Numerical data that is collected, processed, and analyzed as an aid to decision making, such as for those involving demographics of the consumers of a product or quality deviation of samples from a production line.

status quo Generally, the existing state of affairs or that which existed at a particular time. *Law* Of the state that existed before a conflict, and to which condition the court seeks to return the contesting parties.

statute *Law* An ordinance or regulation; a law passed by a legislative body.

statute of limitations *Law* Any law that sets a time during which parties must take action to enforce their rights or forever more forfeit them.

step Any one of a series of related actions.

stet *Let it stand*—a printer's mark to indicate that copy, however otherwise marked, is not to be changed.

steward See *shop steward*.

stewardship Acting in a responsible manner as relates to the preservation, investment, etc. of funds that have been entrusted to ones care.

stiff *Colloq.* To avoid paying or to refuse to pay. That is excessive, as a price or a penalty.

stipend Any periodic payment, as for services, a pension, etc. A salary.

stipulation A reserve clause in a contract *Law* An agreement or concession between parties to a legal proceeding, generally in writing. A stipulation differs from a contract in that it does not require a consideration.

stock *Commerce* Merchandise that is normally kept on hand by a particular business for sale to its clients. *Finance* Shares representing capital investment in a company. *Manufacturing* Raw materials that are to be used in the manufacture or fabrication of a product.

stock certificate *Finance* A document issued as evidence of an equity position in a company.

stockholder *Finance* One who owns shares of stock in a company.

stockholders' equity *Finance* The net worth of a corporation; the value of the stockholders' investment in a company

stock in trade *Commerce* The goods or services that a particular company supplies. The technique, type of service, or style, that is characteristic of a company or its personnel.

stock option *Finance* The right to buy or sell a stock at a certain price within a specified period. *Labor Relations* A type of compensation in which an employee is given the right to buy company stock at a certain price within a specified period. Such plans are normally offered to those in the upper levels of management on the theory that if they do their jobs well, the price of the stock will rise and increase the value of the option.

stockpile *Commerce* To accumulate materials, supplies or finished goods in anticipation of a shortage or price increase.

stock split *Finance* Increasing the number of shares of a company's stock without diluting the equity or earnings of the shareholders by replacing each share with two or more shares that together are worth the same as the original share. A stock split tends to increase trading because it makes the shares more accessible to those who have less to invest.

stonewalling *Colloq.* To be evasive, or to obstruct, as by withholding information.

storage *Computers* The area in a computer, as a hard disk, or an external device, as a diskette or tape, where copies of program and data files are kept for future use.

storage capacity *Computers* The volume of data, expressed in bytes, that can be contained in a storage device.

store *Commerce* An establishment that stocks goods for sale to consumers, or that is the base of operations for the sale of goods or services.

store brand *Marketing* A brand of merchandise that is associated with a particular retailer, and that is prepared, packaged, labeled, etc. to meet the retailer's specifications.

straight-line depreciation *Accounting* The most common form of depreciation for general accounting reports, whereby the annual depreciation for an asset is calculated by deducting salvage value from the cost of the asset and dividing by the anticipated life. For example, a van used in the business is purchased for $20,000 and is expected to have a useful life of five years at the end of which time it will be worth $5,000. Subtracting $5,000, the salvage value, from $20,000, the cost, leaves $15,000 to depreciate; $15,000 divided by five, the number of years over which it is to be depreciated, gives a total of $3,000 per year that may be claimed for depreciation.

straight time Of the standard rate of pay determined by law, company policy, or a collective bargaining agreement, without addition of shift differential, overtime pay, etc.

strategic planning The formulation of a strategy for company operations in terms of products, markets, long-term profitability, etc.

straw boss *Manufacturing* A group leader on a production line, often an individual of limited authority, but who sets the pace of the line.

strike *Labor Relations* Refusal by the members of a bargaining unit in a company to continue working in an attempt to pressure the employer to settle a grievance or reach agreement on a contract. *Law* Any unified action by a group of people calculated to pressure an individual or entity to meet certain demands, as by workers who refuse to work overtime, or tenants who act together in withholding rent until improvements are made.

strike benefits *Labor Relations* Any payment or other assistance to employees who are on strike, as from the union strike fund, food stamps, unemployment compensation, etc.

strikebreaker *Labor Relations* Anyone who accepts employment to replace a worker who is on strike.

string *Computers* A series of characters or symbols processed as a unit.

struck work Goods that are produced by strikebreakers or by a company that contracts with one that is on strike.

structure A building used for the offices or manufacturing plant of a company. The organization of the lines of authority, responsibility and communication throughout the various departments and divisions that make up a company.

subcontractor *Manufacturing* One who accepts the responsibility for producing all or part of a project booked by a principal contractor or another subcontractor. A subcontractor may be engaged to perform work that a primary contractor is too busy to do or a portion of a project that requires special skills or capabilities that the primary contractor does not have. See also *joint venture*.

subliminal advertising *Marketing* Of a visual message projected on a motion picture or television screen in short bursts so that it is received below the level of consciousness, that is without the receiver's awareness. Such messages have been declared illegal.

subsidiary *Finance* A company that is more than fifty percent owned by another company to which it is subordinate.

subsidiary ledger *Accounting* A record of like accounts, as for *accounts receivable*, entered from the *accounts receivable journal* which detail supports the entries to the subsidiary ledger. The entries to the subsidiary ledger, in turn, support the entry to *accounts receivable* in the general ledger.

subsidy Compensation or other incentive paid to individuals, companies, etc. to assist in their continuance or growth, as for the poor, farmers, and certain industries

substandard wage *Labor Relations* A rate of pay that

is below subsistence level, the legal minimum, or the average for a particular business or industry.

substantive law *Law* Statute that defines and regulates rights and duties and that may give right to a cause of action.

substitution effect *Marketing* The theory that a drop in the price of a product will cause buyers to substitute it for another product and that a price increase will cause buyers to look for a substitute.

suffix *Computers* An addendum to a computer file name, separated from the name by a period, that aids in identifying the file contents, as .*SYS* for a system file, .*TXT* for a text file, etc.

suggested retail price *Marketing* The selling price for a product, suggested by the manufacturer.

suggestion system *Labor Relations* A formal procedure whereby employees can offer ideas for improvements in company operations, ranging from a suggestion box where opinions are submitted in writing, to periodic open meetings where those attending are invited to present their ideas to a suggestion panel for consideration, often including a system of cash awards based on the value of the idea.

summarize To abbreviate by discarding unnecessary detail; to condense data by totaling like elements.

sunshine laws *Law* State and federal regulations requiring that certain meetings of regulatory bodies and legislators, and the records of such meetings, be made open to the public.

superfund A federal fund designated for the cleanup of hazardous waste areas.

superintendent An executive responsible for the operation of a manufacturing plant, a department or section within the plant, etc.

Super VGA *Computers* Of a technology that creates a monitor display of higher resolution than VGA.

supervisor Anyone who is directly responsible for overseeing the work of an individual or a group.

supplemental agreement *Law* Anything that is added to a contract to correct a deficiency.

supplemental budget *Accounting* An additional periodic allocation to adjust a budget allowance, such as for additional supplies and labor when the production requirements for a period are greater than anticipated.

supplier One who supplies materials, supplies or services to a manufacturer, or consumer goods to a wholesaler or retailer.

support services *Computers* Ongoing help available to the computer user from hardware or software manufacturers or vendors, usually via a toll free hot line or bulletin board.

surety *Law* One who agrees to guarantee payment for the debts or default of another.

surety bond *Finance* An agreement containing a third party guarantee that damages owed up to a certain amount will be paid if the purchaser of the bond does not fulfill the obligations of a contract. See also *performance bond*.

surge protector *Computers* A device that interfaces between computers or peripherals and their power sources to protect the devices from sudden surges in line voltage.

survey *Marketing* The systematic gathering of information from users in order to learn how to improve a product or service.

survivorship *Law* The right of a person who owns property in joint tenancy with another to full ownership of the property when the other person dies.

suspense account *Accounting* An account used for the temporary recording of a transaction that is not yet clearly defined, on the premise that it is better to have the amount stand out than to record it incorrectly. Payment for an insurance or damage claim, for example, may require study to determine allocation of the amount.

suspension *Labor Relations* A procedural or disciplinary layoff of an employee, usually without pay.

sweat equity *Colloq.* Occasionally of physical improvements to a property made by a proprietor who does his own carpentry, plumbing, etc. Usually of the contribution of long hours and hard work that builds volume and goodwill.

sweatshop *Manufacturing* Descriptive of a business characterized by a labor force that works long hours for low wages under substandard conditions.

sweepstakes *Marketing* A lottery to promote the sale of a product or service, in which participants are not required to wager or to buy, but only to sign up for eligibility to win.

sweetheart contract *Labor Relations* A collective bargaining agreement that is the result of collusion between company management and union officials, and that is not in the best interests of the members of the bargaining unit.

swing shift *Colloq.* The work shift between the day and night, roughly mid-afternoon until around midnight; second shift. Occasionally describing the changing schedule of a worker from shift to shift in a twenty-four hour, seven day a week operation.

switch See *bait and switch*.

symbol *Computers* Any of the characters available from the computer keyboard. A program defined element, as a mark or word, that represents a command or instruction.

symbolic logic *Computers* The use of symbols in a formula to test the relationship between elements.

symbolic name *Computers* A label that identifies a program, a file, a data field, a range of data, etc.

symbolic pricing *Marketing* The establishment of a selling price for a product that is artificially high to place the product in a particular consumer niche.

sympathy strike *Labor Relations* A strike by a union not involved in a dispute, in order to shop solidarity with another union that is involved.

syndicate An association of two or more individuals or companies to share in a project or enterprise, often one that they could not, or would not, attempt singly.

syntax *Computers* The precise structure of a programming language required of one writing instructions for a computer.

synthesizer *Computers* An electronic device for producing sound from digital data.

system Any orderly arrangement of related data, rules, tasks, devices, etc. that serves to form a logical whole.

system backup *Computers* A reserved copy of all of the program and data files in a computer. A second set of hardware that can replace the primary hardware in the event of equipment failure.

system disk *Computers* A disk that contains the basic files the computer needs to operate.

system prompt *Computers* The symbols or characters on a monitor screen that indicate the command line where instructions to the operating system are to be typed.

system resources *Computers* All of the elements unique to a particular computer system, as peripheral devices, type of CPU, memory, etc.

systems analyst *Computers, Manufacturing* One accomplished in the study of complex sets of tasks, especially in a particular area of specialization, and who can recommend means for improvement.

system software *Computers* The programs that control the operation of a computer and the way in which it communicates with peripherals.

table *Computers* An orderly arrangement of related data in rows and columns; a two dimensional array.

table lookup *Computers* To locate a variable as a function of two values in a two dimensional array.

take delivery *Commerce* To personally or through an agent, as a receiving clerk, accept materials, supplies, merchandise, etc. sent by another. To *take delivery* implies that the goods are essentially those that were ordered, that they are acceptable as to condition with any exceptions noted on the bill that was signed to acknowledge delivery, and that the receiver intends to pay for the goods.

takeover The acquisition of one company by another through outright purchase or by acquiring over fifty percent of the outstanding stock of the firm.

tangible asset, tangible property *Accounting, Finance, Law* Descriptive of equity that is corporeal, that is, it can be seen and felt, in contrast to an *intangible asset*, such as a copyright or franchise. In some instances, especially law, *tangible property* refers to personal property, or that which can be carried or moved, in contrast to *real estate* or buildings.

take inventory *Accounting* To count and make a record of all items in storage, as materials, supplies, finished goods, etc., usually at the end of an accounting period to verify the numbers in a *perpetual inventory* and to valuate the inventory or reporting on the financial statements.

take stock Occasionally, to take a physical count of material in inventory. In more common usage, to pause and reflect; to consider a situation carefully before making a decision.

tape backup *Computers* A reserve copy of computer programs and data on magnetic tape.

tape drive *Computers* A device that reads and writes data to magnetic tape for storage, often used for the backup system of a mini or microcomputer.

target market *Marketing* Organizations that fit a particular set of criteria and are therefore viewed as potential buyers for a product or service. Individuals who, because they fit a particular demographic or psychographic profile are considered good prospects for the sale of certain goods or services.

target price *Manufacturing* The cost for which a product must be fabricated in order to conform to the company's profit goals. *Marketing* The price at which a product will find a market, and therefore, the price that includes the cost of the product, advertising, profit, etc. at which it must be brought to market.

tariff *Colloq.* Any bill or charge. *Commerce* A tax on imported goods, or the rate of such tax. The rate schedule for a truck or rail line.

task Generally, work, usually one of a number of acts that make up an undertaking, or sometimes an undertaking involving some difficulty, depending on the context in which it is used.

task management A technique for control that divides a complex job into a series of tasks, each of which is analyzed and revised to achieve optimum performance before integration with other tasks.

tax court *Law* An independent federal agency that hears appeals of disputes between taxpayers and the Internal Revenue Service.

tax deferred *Finance* Of any investment whose earnings are exempt from tax until some time or action in the future.

tax evasion *Law* The deliberate, illegal avoidance of taxes by nonpayment or under payment. *Avoidance* alone is not illegal in that it may designate a legal means of minimizing taxes.

tax exempt *Law* That which is not subject to tax, as the income from interest on state and local bonds.

tax incentive *Finance* Of the nature of certain taxes that encourage investment, as by depreciation allowances, capital gains, etc.

tax planning *Finance* An analysis of tax and investment options in order to determine the best combination of minimize taxes.

tax shelter *Finance, Law* An investment providing tax credits or deductions that can be used to offset other income, thus "sheltering" it from taxes.

tax year Any contiguous twelve month period in the life of a company or other entity, usually a calendar year, although a company may elect to coincide with a fiscal year that begins at any time as long as it does not change from year to year.

team management A system for the administration of a project that places the decision-making in the hands of a group of individuals often with different specialties that compliment each other, and that are necessary to the project. Such a system may be used to develop and implement a marketing plan for a new product or to set up a new plant or production line.

teaser ad *Marketing* An advertisement designed to attract the attention of the public without revealing the product, generally one of a series of ads in a program that culminates in a media blitz promoting the product.

technological unemployment *Labor Relations* The loss of jobs in a business or industry due to advancing technology that has made a product obsolete; that has replaced laborers with machines; or that has changed the character of a job so that those who usually perform certain tasks are no longer qualified.

telecommunications Communication by wire, especially, telephone lines for the transmission of voice, facsimile, and computer data.

telemarketing *Marketing* Use of the telephone for any phase of the promotion and sale of a product, that includes conducting a telephone survey, making an appointment for a salesman to call, ascertaining interest in a product or service so that additional information can be sent through the mail, any attempt to secure an order over the telephone, or the acceptance of orders for merchandise promoted elsewhere, as in print or on television.

tenancy *Law* The right to the possession and use of real estate, as by ownership or lease.

tenancy in common *Law* Ownership of property by two or more persons, with ownership share passing to the heirs of any owner who dies. See also *joint tenancy*.

tenement *Colloq.* A multiple dwelling that offers few amenities, or that is run down. *Law* Generally, any structure attached to the land, or a dwelling place for a tenant.

tenure *Labor Relations* The right of continued employment to one who is gainfully employed by a company or other entity, often by virtue of time in the position, guaranteed by a collective bargaining agreement. See also *seniority*. *Law* A right to hold, as property or a position.

term Generally, a specific length of time or a condition, as for the period that a contract is in force and the contingencies regarding its execution.

terminal *Computers* A device, minimally comprising a

keyboard and a viewing screen, that allows the user to interact with the computer by entering instructions or information and monitoring the processing.

termination *Labor Relations* The conclusion of employment, whether by the employer or employee.

term life insurance *Insurance* An insurance policy paying death benefits that is in force for a specific period, at the end of which time it may be renewed, usually requiring renegotiation of the cost of the protection.

terms *Finance* The details, as interest rate and repayment schedule, of a loan. See also *term*.

territory Generally, of an geographical area; often, referring to the scope of one's expertise or responsibility. *Marketing* Of the geographic area, type of client, etc. that is covered by a salesperson.

test Generally, an examination or trial. *Computers* To subject to diagnostics or sample problems to ascertain that a hardware device or program is working properly. *Manufacturing* Of experimentation with materials, supplies or methods to determine the most effective combination to achieve cost and quality objectives. *Marketing* Of experimentation with advertising or marketing strategies to determine the most economical, effective, or profitable means to sell a product.

testimonial *Marketing* A statement by a well-known personality attesting to the value of a product.

test market *Marketing* An area selected for experimentation with various advertising, pricing, or distribution plans for a product.

text editor *Computer* A type of word processor with limited formatting capabilities, usually used for writing or editing programs

think tank *Colloq.* An organization whose members are engaged in the intensive study and evaluation of problems or projects in order to offer advice to businesses or governmental bodies.

three dimensional array *Computers* An ordered group of like elements, aligned in rows, columns and layers.

three dimensional graphics *Computers* The simulation, on a computer monitor screen, of a three dimensional object.

thrift shop *Marketing* An outlet that specializes in discounted merchandise, often used.

tickler A reminder, or system of reminders, for directing attention to some important matter at an appropriate time, such as a set of dated files in which are stored information about those things that require action by a particular day or week. *Computer* A TSR program for the recording of appointments or other matters of importance, and that pops up at the beginning of a day or at the required time during the day to remind the user of meetings, etc.

tie-in *Marketing* Of special advertising or promotions that are associated with an ongoing campaign. Of a product that is associated in advertising or point-of-sale displays with another, related product, such as featuring a cooler for sale in conjunction with the sale of cold beverages, often with a special price on the purchase of both items.

tight ship Of a company or department that is run

according to a set of strict regulations; often of the supervisor, who is cited as *running a tight ship*.

time and a half *Labor Relations* A reference to the rate of pay for working overtime; of the period worked for that rate. *Law* Pay rate mandated by federal law for working over forty hours in a week.

time and motion study *Manufacturing* A careful examination the time required, and the nature of each worker's movements, to complete a task, or a series of tasks, for the purpose of determining how to make them more efficient and productive.

time card *Manufacturing* A document that records the starting and stopping time for each employee. Often used also to record the times spent on various tasks or jobs during the day as part of a job cost system.

timekeeper *Accounting* One who reviews and records the data from time cards for payroll and cost accounts. Infrequently, one who records the starting and ending times of workers for a company, department or work crew.

time management A program for organizing ones tasks to make the best use of available time.

time-sharing *Computers* A system for utilization of a computer, usually a mainframe, by a number of users. Often a service provided by an outside firm to a number of companies that require the use of a large computer, but cannot justify its purchase. The increasing power and decreasing price of minicomputers has made the practice less common than in the past.

timetable Generally, a schedule of times for the occurrence of certain events, as the arrival and departure of public transportation. *Marketing* A schedule for coordinating specific events in a program of advertising, promotion, introduction of a new product, etc.

title *Law* The right of possession, especially for real estate.

tokenism The practice of hiring a few minority workers to counter claims of discrimination.

top down management A corporate style wherein all decisions are made at the top and then sifted down through the ranks.

topping out Of anything that has reached its peak, as the popularity of a product.

tort *Law* A wrong stemming from an act, or failure to act, in a prudent manner, that is not criminal and that is, however, grounds for a civil suit.

total cost *Accounting* The entire expense, that is, material, labor and overhead, required to fabricate a product.

total debt *Accounting, Finance* The sum of all the money owed by an organization, whether in the short or long term.

total fixed cost *Accounting, Finance* The sum of all expenses for a given period that do not vary with units of production; in effect, the cost to keep the doors of a business open during that period if nothing is produced.

total revenue *Accounting, Finance* The entire amount of income received, or owed, to a company during a given period, from any source and for any purpose.

touch terminal *Computers* A device that allows the selection of options or entry of data by touching areas of a computer monitor screen.

tour *Labor Relations* Of the hours an employee is scheduled to work. Occasionally of the time spent working for a company by one is no longer employed there.

tout *Colloq. Marketing* To promote or extol the virtues of a product.

tracer tracking *Commerce* An inquiry or effort to seek the whereabouts of a lost package or shipment.

trackball *Computers* A hand held device similar to a *mouse* but with a fixed base holding a sphere that is manipulated to move the cursor.

tractor feed *Computers* Of a device that guides continuous-feed paper through a printer using holes that are punched into strips along the side of the paper.

trade *Commerce* Collectively all those engaged in a similar business of line of work. *Manufacturing* Generally a means of making a living; an occupation. Once used to refer only to skilled workers.

trade advertising *Marketing* Advertising and promotion that targets industrial users of a product.

trade association An alliance of those engaged in the same or closely related lines of business usually formed for the pursuit of any cause that is seen to be in the best interests of its members, as for education and training, public relations, influencing legislation, etc.

trade magazine A periodical that is directed to the interests of those in a particular line of business.

trademark A design, symbol, etc. usually protected by registration, used by a company to distinguish its products or services from those of its competitors.

trade name The name used by a company for doing business that is not necessarily the name under which the corporation is organized; see also *dba*. A name used by a company for its products or services; a trademark.

trade reference *Accounting* The name of a company doing business with a prospective buyer; given to a seller by the buyer as a credit reference and often in the same business as the seller.

trade secret Information about a technique, device, etc. that affords a company a competitive advantage and that in the hands of a competitor would work to cause harm to the company.

trade show A gathering of exhibitors whose purpose is to display and promote their products and services to prospective buyers who represent companies in related lines of business.

trade union *Labor Relations* Originally an association of those engaged in a particular craft; now generally used to designate any labor union.

transaction Any activity associated with trading or the carrying on of business; a business deal. *Law* The completion of any arrangement related to business between two or more persons.

transaction file *Accounting Computers* A record of recent transactions used to update a master file such as a record of daily sales used to update the sales account, receivables, cash account, inventory, etc.

transaction terminal *Computers* A device that permits remote input of data directly to the computer such as on a shop floor or at a cash register.

transfer *Computers* To move data or files from one location, storage device, or computer to another.

transient Temporary; passing or changing with time. *Computers* Interim, as a file that is created by a program while it is processing, then deleted when processing is completed. *Finance* Of an upswing or downturn in business that is temporary. *Labor Relations* Of the work force in a seasonal business.

translate *Computers* To convert data from one format or program to another. To convert signals from one format to another as from analog to digital input.

transmission *Computers* The transfer of signals between elements of a computer system.

transmission speed *Computers* The rate at which data can be sent and received.

transmittal *Finance* A document that lists items being transferred and that serves as verification of the transfer, such as for negotiable instruments, stock certificates, etc. especially for materials that are not ordinarily copied.

transparent *Computers* Descriptive of computer processing that is taking place in the background not under the direct supervision of or apparent to the user.

transportation *Commerce* Any conveyance for moving people or things. Collectively of a type of conveyance or all means of conveyance.

travel and entertainment *Accounting Marketing* The expenses usually associated with sales or marketing activities that are incurred for travel to visit clients, attend trade shows, etc. and for the entertaining of clients in the normal course of business.

treasurer *Finance* The officer who is responsible for management of the funds of an organization and, in a public corporation, for maintaining a market in its securities.

treasury stock *Finance* Shares of a company's stock that have been bought back by the company.

tree diagram A graphic representation of a tree-like structure that shows the relationship of positions in a corporation, a sequence of events, the directory structure of computer files, etc. that emanates from a single point and branches out through various levels, depicted inverted so that the point of origin is at the top of the diagram.

trend Of conditions or events with a tendency to continue in a particular direction, as for style changes, the movement of sales, or cost increases. Recognizing and coping with trends is an important factor in long range planning.

trespass *Law* Interference with the rights of an owner to use property as he or she sees fit. Such trespass may be entry onto the land by the trespasser, the removal of property, or the depositing of property as trash.

trial and error Problem solving by attempting a solution and observing the results; often used in test marketing to determine the best means to promote a product.

trial balance *Accounting* A worksheet that is a listing of ledger accounts at the end of an accounting period to be sure that all balance prior to closing the books.

trial offer *Marketing* A proposal to a prospective buyer that permits the use or inspection of a product without charge for a specified period; a technique for getting the attention of first time buyers.

troubleshooter *Colloq.* One who specializes in analyzing and solving problems.

truncation Generally, the contraction of a number by cutting off a non significant portion. *Computers* The compression of a result of calculation that is too long for a program to record.

truth in lending *Law* Federal regulation requiring that those applying for credit be given comprehensive information about the dollar amount and the annual rate of the interest. In addition, when real property is pledged as security, the buyer must be allowed three working days in which to cancel the transaction.

TSR, terminate and stay resident *Computers* Of a utility program, such as an appointment calendar, that can be loaded into memory and called up as needed.

turkey *Colloq.* Of something that does not perform to expectations, as an investment or a person.

turnaround, turn the corner *Colloq.* An improvement in the fortunes of a company, a venture, or an operation.

turnkey *Computers, Manufacturing* Of a system or other project that is designed to the client's specifications and that is thoroughly tested and ready to operate before being turned over to the client.

turnover *Labor Relations* Of the rate of change in the labor force, often a measure of worker satisfaction, effectiveness of the selection and screening process, etc. *Marketing* Of the frequency with which the product moves from the shelves to the consumer.

tutorial *Computers* An adjunct to a program that teaches the user how to use the program.

two dimensional array *Computers* An ordered group of like elements, formed in rows and columns.

tycoon A person of wealth and power who is prominent in industry or in financial circles.

type ahead buffer *Computers* An area of memory that stores key strokes entered faster than they can be processed.

ultra vires *Latin* Beyond the power of. *Law* Of corporate action or involvement that is outside the realm of activities specified in its charter, and that may give rise to action for withdrawal of its charter.

unauthorized strike *Labor Relations* Any form of strike, as a walkout, work slowdown, refusal to work overtime, etc. by members of a bargaining unit that has not been duly sanctioned by their union.

unbundle *Computers* To separately price, and offer for sale, the various parts, as a computer, monitor, keyboard, printer, programs, etc., of a system that are normally sold as a unit. *Marketing* To break down the invoice from an advertising or promotional agency, such as for charges to place advertisements in various media, creative and design costs, artwork, copy preparation, etc.

uncollected funds *Finance* Of capital that has been pledged and not yet paid, such as for checks that have been drawn, but that have not yet been charged against the account from which drawn.

underapplied *Accounting* Of charges that have not

been fully recovered, such as for overhead in a cost accounting system. For example, if overhead were allocated on the basis of the number of units produced or the number of operating hours, any reduction in units produced or hours of operation would leave a portion of overhead cost that is not applied to the cost of the product. A similar situation occurs when the actual cost of overhead exceeds that on which the budget and allocation of overhead is based.

underabsorption See *underapplied*.

underemployed *Labor Relations* Of one who is engaged in a type of work that does not require his or her level of education, experience, or competence, a condition that often exists when there are more workers than there are available jobs. Within a company, a worker faced with layoff may exercise the right to bump another with less seniority, and thus wind up with a lower level job. *Manufacturing* Of a plant, production line, machine, etc. that is not being fully utilized.

underground economy Descriptive of activity that is not reported for tax purposes, such as bartering for goods or services, payments off the books, or dealing in illegal substances.

underpaid *Labor Relations* Of one who has been shorted in a particular pay period, such as for an error in reported hours, wage rate, etc. Of one who is working for a wage that is less than the legal rate, that originally agreed to by the employer, that specified in a contract, or that which is the normal rate for the job in that market.

under the counter Of payment that is made off the books, or not recorded. Such payment may be to simply avoid the paperwork involved in putting a casual worker on the payroll, but more often the term is used to describe payments that are illegal, as for a bribe or to avoid taxes.

undervalued *Accounting* Of an asset that is carried on the books at a figure that is far less than its true worth. *Finance* Of a security, as a company stock, that is trading at less than its apparent worth, often because of a slow market.

undiscounted list *Marketing* Of a published schedule of prices that shows only the full wholesale or retail rates for merchandise. Such lists, or catalogs, are often prepared by a manufacturer or wholesaler for wide distribution; individual distributors or merchants are then assigned a discount rate at which they may purchase.

undivided interest *Law* In property that is jointly owned, the right of each of the owners to use and possession of the entire property. The right to profits from the property, or proceeds from its sale, are shared according to each owner's undivided interest, but each has a right to possession of the whole.

undue influence *Law* Control or authority wielded by one party to a transaction over the other and that transcends the free will of the other in relation to the transaction.

unearned income *Accounting* Advance payments for which goods or services have not yet been furnished. *Finance* For tax purposes, income for other than personal services, as investment or interest income.

unemployable *Labor Relations* Generally, of one who is habitually unemployed, often for lack of skill or education, or because of inability to adjust to the restrictions imposed by most jobs, as by arriving on time every day. Many such *unemployables* are simply unsuited to the type of jobs they have been seeking, or that are available in their market area.

unemployment Generally, the state of not being used. The condition of being without steady work to provide income or the percentage of those who are without work.

unemployment compensation *Labor Relations* Any payment to subsidize those who are out of work. The federal and state programs that offer regular payments over a set period of time to those without work.

unencumbered *Finance* Of an asset that is owned free and clear, without *lien.*

unfair competition *Law, Marketing* Any attempt in advertising to mislead or defraud a buyer, such as by misrepresenting the cost or quality of a product, by representing a product as that of another, by infringing on the patents or copyrights of another, etc.

unfair labor practice *Labor Relations, Law* Any action of an employer or a labor union that restricts the rights of any member of a bargaining unit, as by coercion, discrimination, refusal to bargain, etc.

Uniform Commercial Code *Commerce* A set of rules adopted by most states to standardize the regulation of transactions involving the sale of merchandise, shipping documents, negotiable instruments, stock transfers, etc.

uninterruptible power supply *Computers* A sophisticated backup power supply that automatically furnishes power to a computer system when the primary power source is interrupted, permitting continued operation or an orderly shutdown.

union See *labor union.*

union shop *Labor Relations* An organization where workers are required to be members of a union; nonunion workers may be hired but are required to join the union within a specified period as a condition of continued employment, a practice outlawed in several states. See also *closed shop open shop right to work.*

unit cost *Accounting* The expenditure for one unit of production including cost for materials, labor, and overhead.

Universal Product Code A distinctive number set that identifies a specific product, represented as a bar code for use with an automated system that records sales, adjusts inventory, etc.

unjust enrichment *Law* Of the principle in law that requires one who has profited unfairly at the expense of another to make restitution.

unrecorded expense *Accounting* Of a cost that has been incurred but not recognized at the end of an accounting period, usually because an invoice was not received.

unrecovered cost *Accounting* In a cost accounting system, an expense that has not been properly matched to the activity that produced it.

unsecured *Finance* Of a loan or debt that does not have an asset pledged as collateral for payment.

unskilled *Labor Relations* Descriptive of a worker who does not possess any special abilities, or a job that does not require special knowledge or training.

up and running *Computers* Descriptive of computers and peripherals that are on line and functioning properly.

update Generally, to add new information. A document, report, etc. that contains the latest information available. *Computers* Of a newer version of an existing program that offers new features, or corrects problems in the original version.

up front *Accounting* Of that which is paid or takes place in advance, as the down payment on an order.

upgrade An improvement, as of quality. *Marketing* Of a sale in which the buyer is moved to the purchase of a larger quantity, of better quality, etc.

upkeep *Manufacturing* Of the care and maintenance of equipment.

upscale *Marketing* Generally, descriptive of those products or markets characterized by higher than average prices, and often, better quality.

upswing *Finance* A change toward increased demand for a product, or an improvement in the economy as a whole.

up time *Computers* The period that a computer is on line and functioning properly.

upward compatibility *Computers* Descriptive of features built into a computer that permit upgrading.

upwardly mobile *Marketing* Descriptive of a demographic group that is likely to experience a steady improvement in status, income, standard of living, etc.

useful life

useful life *Accounting* The length of time before an asset costs more to keep in operating condition than it earns.

user friendly *Computer* Of an operating system or program that requires minimal training of users and that is intuitive, making use easier.

user group *Computers* A special interest group that meets to share information about a particular program, or computers in general.

user hot line *Computers* A telephone number provided by an equipment or software manufacturer or dealer through which a user may access technical help.

usury The practice of loaning money at an excessive rate of interest. *Law* Interest that is excessive and perhaps unlawful.

utility The quality of being useful; that which is useful. *Accounting* Generally the expenses for public utilities as gas, water, electricity, etc. *Computers* A program that assists in the operation or management of the computer, peripheral devices, or other programs, etc.

utter *Law* The passing or attempt to pass a forged instrument, as a check.

vacation pay *Labor Relations* Income paid to an employee for the time he or she is on vacation, usually one to four weeks a year depending on the employee's length of service.

valid Descriptive of that which is recognized as having legal force.

valuable consideration *Law* Inducement for a contract; something of value given to fulfill a contractual obligation.

valuation An estimate of the worth or cost of a thing, as a machine.

value The equivalent worth of a thing in money or some other medium of exchange. *Accounting* The amount at which assets are recorded and reported. *Marketing* The price at which goods are sold. The relative worth of goods to a buyer.

value added *Accounting* The amount by which the cost of goods are increased as the result of processing; a system that accounts for such cost. *Finance* The contribution to the worth of goods by a manufacturer or fabricator, determined by the difference between the cost of materials and the selling price.

value judgment An estimate of a situation, worth, etc. based on insight and intuition.

variable That which is subject to change. *Accounting* Descriptive of expenses that change with level of activity. *Computers* An element in a program that varies with input. *Marketing* Descriptive of those things that can affect the demand for a product.

variable budget *Accounting* A scale listing anticipated cost for various levels of output or activity. A schedule of those expenses that change with the level of volume or activity.

variable cost *Accounting* Cost, as labor and materials, associated with a unit of production and that varies directly with the number of units produced. Cost, such as floor supervision, that may vary with the level of production, but not directly with the number of units produced; also called semi-variable cost.

variable expense *Accounting* Expenses that change with the level of activity or production.

variable interest rate *Finance* A charge for the use of borrowed money that, by agreement, may be changed over the life of a loan, with the change usually pegged to some index.

variable name *Computers* A label that represents an element that can assume a changing value, such as a range of cells in a spreadsheet.

variable pricing *Marketing* The practice of charging different prices to different buyers, usually at the retail level, where a buyer and seller may haggle over price. On the wholesale level, variable pricing may exist, but usually must be based on some cost factor, such as packaging, volume, etc.

variance Generally, the qualification or quantification of difference. *Accounting* The difference between budgeted and actual expenses, sales, earnings, etc. *Law* In zoning, exemption from a zoning ordinance granted by the appropriate authority to one who would suffer undue and unnecessary hardship if the ordinance were strictly enforced.

vendor Generally, one who sells; a supplier of goods or services.

venture An endeavor that implies an element of risk, as in starting a business where the possibility of loss exists with the possibility of gain.

venture capital *Finance* Money or other assets loaned to start a business or invested in a business. Such loans often carry an interest rate that is higher than that for a going business in recognition of the extra element of risk.

vertical integration The expansion of a company into a new level or levels related to the manufacturing and distribution of its primary products. A manufacturer of furniture, for example, may acquire a company that supplies lumber or fabric for the furniture, or may set up a chain of retail stores to sell the furniture. See also *horizontal integration.*

vested *Law* Absolute, as of a right that is not contingent on any act or event.

vested rights *Labor Relations* Of the absolute claim of an employee to the benefits of a pension plan at normal retirement age or to election of a lump sum payment as provided for in the plan if separated from the company prior to retirement. Vesting generally requires a minimum time of service with the company sponsoring the plan.

VGA, Video Graphics Array *Computers* A standard for high resolution display on a color monitor screen.

vicarious liability *Law* Responsibility placed on one for the actions of another, as a damage claim against an employer for injury caused by his or her employee while on the job. See also *imputed liability.*

video card *Computers* A board in the computer that controls the display on the monitor.

violation *Law* An act that is disruptive to normal order, or contrary to law.

virtual memory *Computers* An extension of the computer's main memory in disk storage.

virus *Computers* Unauthorized instructions in the computer that disrupt its normal operation.

vocabulary *Computers* The collection of reserved words that are acceptable for use in a particular programming language.

vocational rehabilitation *Labor Relations* A program

for upgrading skills or learning new ones so as to be more employable, such as a company program for retraining employees who have been displaced by automation.

voice activated *Computers* Of a computer or computer program that responds to voice commands.

void *Law* Having no legal force; invalid.

voidable *Law* Of a contract that is defective and that may be canceled without recourse.

volatile Descriptive of that which may change quickly and unexpectedly, as a particular market in goods, or the tone of labor negotiations. *Computers* Of memory that must be constantly refreshed to be retained and that is erased when the power is off.

volume A quantity or amount, as of the number of units produced, or the dollar amount of business.

volume discount *Marketing* A price reduction, or special price, based on the number of units purchased.

voluntary bankruptcy *Finance, Law* An action wherein a company or other entity that is insolvent petitions the court for protection from its creditors in anticipation that, operating under the direction of the court, it may preserve its assets for the benefit of creditors and stockholders alike.

voting stock *Finance* Shares in a company that entitle the shareholder to a single vote in corporate elections for each share of stock held.

voucher *Accounting* A form used for the control of the processing of charges and disbursements: invoices received from vendors are assigned numbered vouchers which record necessary data about the invoice required for processing and payment. *Commerce* A document that serves as evidence to a transaction, or authority to make such a transaction, such as for the receipt or shipment of goods.

wage The amount of money paid an employee for work, usually based on an hourly rate.

wage bracket The range of wage rates or salaries paid for a particular type of work.

wage scale A listing of the wages paid for all of the jobs or job levels covered by a collective bargaining agreement or by company policy.

waiver *Law* The voluntary relinquishing of a right; a document attesting to such relinquishing.

waiver of premium *Insurance* A provision in an insurance policy as for illness or disability that keeps the policy in force without payment of further premiums.

walkout Generally, a sudden departure to protest, as for those attending a meeting. *Labor Relations* A strike by workers to protest a contract violation, pressure for settlement of a grievance, etc.

want ad *Colloq.* A classified advertisement in the newspaper, especially those listing opportunities for employment.

warehouse receipt *Law* A formal document of title that is a receipt for goods, issued by a person or business that deals in the storage of such goods. In certain cases a warehouse receipt may be a negotiable instrument in that it entitles the bearer to possession of the goods it lists and that its sale constitutes delivery of those goods.

warranty *Insurance* Assurance by one who is

contracting for protection that conditions related to the risk are as stated or will be amended to conform such as for the installation of smoke alarms or a sprinkler system. *Law* A guarantee that property or goods described in a contract are correctly represented and that they will be replaced or repaired if found deficient. *Marketing* A guarantee to a consumer of the quality of merchandise for sale usually with provision for repair or replacement of defective items within a specified period from the date of purchase.

waste *Law* Improper use or negligence of land by one rightfully in possession that significantly reduces the value to another who owns an interest in the land. *Manufacturing* Material that is no longer useful; a byproduct of fabrication to be discarded.

wasted circulation *Marketing* Advertising in a market where a product is not available.

waybill *Commerce* A document that accompanies a shipment of goods listing the shipper destination routing and a description of the goods being conveyed.

wealth Generally of anything in profusion. *Finance* Collectively the monetary value of the assets belonging to a person business country etc.

wear and tear *Accounting* Descriptive of the normal use of a product that causes a reduction in its value over time.

white collar crime *Colloq.* Designating of illegal acts by one in a position of responsibility such as stock fraud bribery or embezzlement.

white collar worker *Colloq.* Generally descriptive of

one who works in an office or at a profession.

white elephant Generally of that which is of no value to its owner, often maintained at great expense and occasionally of that which may have value to another.

wholesaler *Commerce* Usually one who buys from a manufacturer in very large quantities and sells to retailers in somewhat smaller lots.

wildcat strike See *unauthorized strike*.

windfall windfall profit *Accounting* An often sudden, unexpected benefit as by the purchase of materials or goods for resale at an especially low price.

window *Computers* A viewing area on a computer monitor screen.

window dressing *Accounting Finance* Any information or presentation of financial data that makes results appear better than they are. *Marketing* Packaging a product in such a way as to make it appear more valuable than it is.

withholding *Accounting* The amounts held back from a worker's wage or salary for income taxes, insurance, union dues, etc.

word processor *Computers* A small computer with self-contained monitor and printer that is designed to function as a typewriter, used to generate correspondence, reports, etc. often with a spelling or grammar checker and the ability to save data to memory built into the machine or on a floppy disk. A computer program designed for the production of typeset documents often with a variety of features or the capacity to add them, such as a spell and grammar checker, insertion and editing of graphics, a large collection of type fonts, etc.

word wrap *Computers* A feature of a word processor or word processor program that provides for the continuation of copy on a new line when one line is filled, relieving the user of the need to manually divide the lines of copy.

workaholic *Colloq.* One who is obsessive about work or abnormally attached to keeping busy.

work experience Collectively, one's knowledge and talents. A list of previous employers usually asked of prospective employees, and including such information as dates of employment, wage rate, reason for leaving, etc.

work flow *Manufacturing* Generally of the path that materials work in process and finished goods follow through the various stages of production. A diagram or graphic representation of the progress of product in a manufacturing operation.

work force, workforce Collectively, all of those employed or available for employment, as to a company or other entity, throughout a geographic area, etc.

working capital *Accounting Finance* The excess of current assets such as cash, accounts receivable, inventory, etc. over current liabilities, those obligations owing and due within one year. Sometimes descriptive of only assets that can be used to pay or pledge for current obligations, such as cash and accounts receivable.

working poor Those who work for minimum wage earning just enough to buy necessities and who lack to education or skills to improve their lot.

work in process work in progress *Accounting* An

item of inventory that represents the labor and material costs assigned to goods that are not completed. *Manufacturing* Product for which fabrication has not yet begun or is only partly completed, representing the workload ahead of a department or operation.

workload *Manufacturing* Collectively, all of the work that has yet to be completed, often within a specified period. The specific work assigned to a person, machine, assembly line, etc., or the amount of such work that can be completed by the entity.

workmen's compensation *Insurance* A state mandated insurance that reimburses workers injured on the job. Requirements vary from state to state, but generally the worker is reimbursed for medical expense, disability and lost wages.

work order *Manufacturing* A document for tracking work through a plant, that contains the identity of the customer, a description of the work, and detailed instructions for its completion. A request to a service department to perform a specific task, as for maintenance on a machine.

work permit *Labor Relations* A document that authorizes a legal alien to work for a specific period of time.

work rules *Labor Relations* Regulations regarding conditions in the workplace, conduct expected of employees and supervisors, etc., often part of a collective bargaining agreement. Sometimes, rules set forth by the company governing procedures, as for safety, tardiness, reporting of injuries, etc.

worksheet *Accounting* A collection of preliminary data

to be used in the preparation of financial reports; a spreadsheet or trial balance.

work simplification *Manufacturing* The process of studying production methods in order to reduce the time, effort, and cost to produce a product or perform a task.

work station *Computers* One of a number of desktop computers or terminals that are linked to other users, a mainframe minicomputer, or file server and peripherals such as printers, plotters, etc. *Manufacturer* Any of a number of points on an assembly line where a worker is positioned to perform some task involved in the fabrication of a product.

work stoppage *Labor Relations* A protest, usually by a group of workers in concert; a *strike* or *walkout*.

worth *Finance* The value of an asset. *Labor Relations* A measure of a worker's contribution to the value of a manufactured product or a service. The comparable value of the services of a particular worker, or of any worker doing a particular job.

writ *Law* A legal document that directs one in a course of action.

write protected *Computers* Descriptive of a storage disk or other device that may be accessed but not changed. See also *read-only*.

WYSIWYG what you see is what you get *Computers* Descriptive of an accurate representation of type and graphics on a monitor screen.

year-end *Accounting Finance* The end of an accounting period that is often, but not necessarily, the end of a calendar year. See also *fiscal year*.

year-to-date *Accounting* The sum of the accounting

periods from the beginning of the current *fiscal year* until the end of the most recent accounting period, usually in reference to accumulated amounts, as sales, expenses, etc.

yellow dog contract *Labor Relations* A contract between an employer and employee that contains a provision precluding membership in a labor union. Such a contract is prohibited in most states and not enforceable in federal courts.

yes man *Colloq.* One who always strives to agree with his or her superiors; a toady.

zero defects A program designed to promote a disposition toward perfection in performance among employees, often with a system of rewards for excellence.

zip code A post office system of numbering delivery areas in order to speed the sorting of mail.

zone Any area, specifically bounded, that is distinct from others in some way.

zoning The dividing of a geographical area into distinct sections, as of a city, usually to restrict their use.

zoning ordinance *Law* A regulation that limits the use of a section of land to specific purpose or bars certain activities in the section, as land set aside for residential dwellings that prohibits industrial development.

Reference Section

International Time Zones

Following is a list of times in cities throughout the world when it is 12 noon Eastern Standard Time in the United States.

Addis Ababa	8 PM
Alexandria	7 PM
Amsterdam	6 PM
Athens	7 PM
Baghdad	8 PM
Bangkok	12 M
Barcelona	5 PM
Beijing	1 AM

(morning of the following day)

Belfast	5 PM
Belgrade	6 PM
Berlin	6 PM
Bogota	12 N
Bombay	10:30 PM
Brasilia	2 PM
Brussels	6 PM
Bucharest	7 PM
Budapest	6 PM
Buenos Aires	2 PM
Cairo	7 PM
Calcutta	10:30 PM
Calgary	10 AM
Cape Town	7 PM
Caracas	1 PM
Casablanca	5 PM
Copenhagen	6 PM
Delhi	10:30 PM

Dublin	5 PM
Edinburgh	5 PM
Florence	6 PM
Frankfurt	6 PM
Geneva	6 PM
Glasgow	5 PM
Halifax	1 PM
Hanoi	1 AM
(morning of the following day)	
Havana	12 N
Helsinki	7 PM
Ho Chi Minh City	1 AM
(morning of the following day)	
Hong Kong	1 AM
(morning of the following day)	
Istanbul	7 PM
Jakarta	12 M
Jerusalem	7 PM
Johannesburg	7 PM
Karachi	10 PM
Kuala Lumpur	1 AM
(morning of the following day)	
Lima	12 N
Lisbon	5 PM
Liverpool	4 PM
London	5 PM
Madrid	5 PM
Managua	11 AM

Manila .... 1 AM
(morning of the following day)
Marseilles .... 6 PM
Mecca .... 8 PM
Melbourne .... 4 AM
(morning of the following day)
Mexico City .... 11 AM
Montreal .... 12 N
Moscow .... 8 PM
Munich .... 6 PM
Naples .... 6 PM
Oslo .... 6 PM
Ottawa .... 12 N
Panama .... 12 N
Paris .... 6 PM
Prague .... 6 PM
Quebec .... 12 N
Rio de Janeiro .... 2 PM
Riyadh .... 8 PM
Rome .... 6 PM
St. Petersburg .... 8 PM
San Juan .... 1 PM
Santiago .... 1 PM
Seoul .... 2 AM
(morning of the following day)
Shanghai .... 1 AM
(morning of the following day)
Stockholm .... 6 PM
Sydney .... 4 AM
(morning of the following day)

Tangiers	5 PM
Teheran	8:30 PM
Tel Aviv	7 PM
Tokyo	2 AM
(morning of the following day)	
Toronto	12 N
Tripoli	7 PM
Vancouver	9 AM
Venice	6 PM
Vienna	6 PM
Vladivostock	3 AM
(morning of the following day)	
Warsaw	6 PM
Winnipeg	11 AM
Yangon	11:30 PM
Yokohama	2 AM
(morning of the following day)	
Zurich	6 PM

Standard Business Abbreviations

abbr. abbreviation
abs. abstract
acct. account
A.D. *anno Domini* in the year of our Lord
ADP automated data processing
AID Agency for International Development
a.k.a. also known as
A.M. or **M.A.** master of arts
a.m. *ante meridiem* before noon
approx. approximately
ave. avenue
B.C. before Christ
bf. boldface
bldg. building
blvd. boulevard
b.o. buyer's option
B.S. or **B.Sc.** bachelor of science
ca. *circa* about
CACM Central American Common Market
c. and s.c. caps and small caps
c.b.d. cash before delivery
C.C.P.A. Court of Customs and Patents Appeals
CEA Council of Economic Advisers
Cento Central Treaty Organization
CEO Chief Executive Officer
cf. confer; compare or see
CO commanding officer; chief of operations
co. company
c.o.d. cash on delivery
Comsat communication satellite
cont. continued
corp. corporation

309

c.p. chemically pure
C.P.A. certified public accountant
CPI Consumer Price Index
cr. credit; creditor
d.b.a. doing business as
dr. debit; debtor; drive
Dr. doctor
E. east
EEC European Economic Community
(Common Market)
EEOC Equal Employment Opportunity Commission
EFrA European Free Trade Association
EFTS electronic funds transfer system
e.g. exempli gratia for example
e.o.m. end of month
EPA Environmental Protection Agency
et al. *et alii* and others
et seq. *et sequential* and the following
etc. *et cetera* and so forth
Euratom European Atomic Energy Community
Eurodollars U.S. dollars used to finance foreign
trade
Euromarket European Common Market,
European Economic Community
f., ff. and following page (pages)
f.a.s. free alongside ship
FDIC Federal Deposit Insurance Corporation
FICA Federal Insurance Contributions Act
FLSA Fair Labor Standards Act
f.o.b. free on board
FPC Federal Power Commission
FRS Federal Reserve System
FSLIC Federal Savings and Loan Insurance Corporation

FTC Federal Trade Commission

GATT General Agreement of Tariffs and Trade

gr. wt. gross weight

ibid. *ibidem* in the same place

ICC Interstate Commerce Commission

id. *idem* the same

i.e. *id est* that is

IMF International Monetary Fund

Inc. incorporated

Interpol International Criminal Police Organization

IOU I owe you

ITO International Trade Organization

Jr. junior

LAFTA Latin American Free Trade Association

lat. latitude

lc. lowercase

liq. liquid

lf. lightface

LL.B. bachelor of laws

LL.D. doctor of laws

loc. cit. *loco citato* in the place cited

long. longitude

Ltd. limited

M. monsieur; **MM.** messieurs

m. *meridies* noon

M.D. doctor of medicine

memo memorandum

MFN most favored nation

Mlle. mademoiselle

Mme. madam

Mmes. mesdames

mo. month

Mr. mister; *plural* Messrs.

Mrs. mistress

Ms. general feminine title; *plural* Mses.
ms., mss. manuscript manuscripts
Msgr. monsignor
MTN multilateral trade negotiations
N. north
NA. not available; not applicable
NAFTA North American Free Trade Agreement
NE. northeast
n.e.c. not elsewhere classified
n.e.s. not elsewhere specified
net wt. net weight
NLRB National Labor Relations Board
No., Nos. number numbers
n.o.p. not otherwise provided (for)
n.o.s. not otherwise specified
n.s.p.f. not specifically provided for
NW. northwest
OAS Organization of American States
op. cit. *opere citato* in the work cited
OPEC Organization of Petroleum Exporting Countries
OTC Organization for Trade Cooperation
PA public accountant; public address (system)
PIN personal identification number
Pl. place
p.m. *post meridiem* afternoon
Prof. professor
pro tem *pro tempore* temporarily
P.S. *post scriptum* postscript; public school
QT on the quiet
R&D research and development
rd. road
Rev. reverend
RR. railroad

Standard Business Abbreviations (cont.)

Rt. Rev. right reverend

Ry. railway

S. south

SAE Society of Automotive Engineers

S&L savings and loan

SBA Small Business Administration

sc. *scilicet* namely (also **ss**)

s.c. small caps

s.d. *sine die* without date

SE. southeast

SEC Securities and Exchange Commission

SOP standard operating procedure

Sq. square

Sr. senior

St., Ste., SS. Saint, Sainte, Saints

st. street

stat. statutes

supt. superintendent

SW. southwest

T., Tps. township, townships

Ter. terrace

uc. uppercase

U.N. United Nations

v., vs. *versus* against

VAT value added tax

VCR video cassette recorder

viz *videlicet* namely

W. west

wf wrong font

WHO World Health Organization

w.o.p. without pay

International Currencies

Following are basic units of currency from around the world. Although some currency names are common to a number of areas it should not be assumed that they are necessarily interchangeable or of equal value.

Afghanistan	afghani
Albania	lek
Algeria	dinar
Angola	kwanza
Argentina	austral
Australia	dollar
Austria	schilling
Bahamas	dollar
Bahrain	dinar
Bangladesh	taka
Barbados	dollar
Belgium	franc
Belize	dollar
Benin	franc
Bhutan	ngultrum
Botswana	pula.
Brunei	dollar
Bulgaria	lev
Burkina Faso	franc
Burundi	franc
Cambodia	riel
Cameroon	franc
Canada	dollar
Cape Verde	escudo
Cayman Islands	dollar
Central Africa	franc
Chad	franc
Chile	peso

China	yuan
Colombia	peso
Comoros	franc
Congo	franc
Costa Rica	colon
Cuba	peso
Cyprus	pound
Denmark	krone
Djibouti	franc
Dominican Republic	peso
Ecuador	sucre
Egypt	pound
El Salvador	colon
Ethiopia	birr
Fiji	dollar
France	franc
Gabon	franc
Gambia	dalasi
Germany	mark
Ghana	cedi
Greece	drachma
Grenada	dollar
Guatemala	quetzal
Guinea-Bissau	peso
Guyana	dollar
Haiti	gourde
Honduras	lempira
Hong Kong	dollar
Hungary	forint
Iceland	krona
India	rupee
Indonesia	rupiah
Iran	rial
Iraq	dinar

Ireland	pound
Israel	shekel
Italy	lira
Ivory Coast	franc
Jamaica	dollar
Japan	yen
Jordan	dinar
Kenya	shilling
Kiribati	dollar
Kuwait	dinar
Laos	kip
Lebanon	pound
Lesotho	loti
Liberia	dollar
Libya	dinar
Liechtenstein	franc
Luxembourg	franc
Madagascar	franc
Mali	franc
Mauritania	ouguiya
Mauritius	rupee
Mexico	peso
Monaco	franc
Mongolia	tugrik
Morocco	dirham
Mozambique	metical
Nauru	dollar
Nepal	rupee
Netherlands	guilder
New Zealand	dollar
Niger	franc
Nigeria	naira
North Korea	won
Norway	krone

Pakistan	rupee
Panama	balboa
Papua New Guinea	kina
Paraguay	guarani
Peru	inti
Philippines	peso
Poland	zloty
Portugal	escudo
Qatar	riyal
Romania	leu
Rwanda	franc
St. Lucia	dollar
St. Vincent and the	
San Marino	lira
Sao Tome	dobra
Saudi Arabia	riyal
Senegal	franc
Seychelles	rupee
Sierra Leone	leone
Singapore	dollar
Solomon Islands	dollar
Somalia	shilling
South Africa	rand
South Korea	won
Spain	peseta
Sri Lanka	rupee
Sudan	pound
Suriname	guilder
Swaziland	lilangeni
Sweden	krona
Switzerland	franc
Syria	pound
Tanzania	shilling
Thailand	baht

International Currencies (cont.)

Togo	franc
Trinidad and Tobago	dollar
Tunisia	dinar
Turkey	lira
Tuvalu	dollar
Uganda	shilling
United Kingdom	pound
United States	dollar
Uruguay	peso
Vanuatu	vatu
Vatican City	lira
Venezuela	bolivar
Vietnam	dong
Western Samoa	tala
Yemen (South?)	dinar
Zaire	zaire
Zambia	kwacha
Zimbabwe	dollar